From the Files of a
SECURITY EXPERT WITNESS

From the Files of a
SECURITY EXPERT WITNESS

CHARLES A. SENNEWALD

ELSEVIER

Amsterdam • Boston • Heidelberg • London • New York • Oxford
Paris • San Diego • San Francisco • Singapore • Sydney • Tokyo
Butterworth-Heinemann is an imprint of Elsevier

Acquiring Editor: Brian Romer
Development Editor: Amber Hodge
Project Manager: Punithavathy Govindaradjane
Designer: Russell Purdy

Butterworth-Heinemann is an imprint of Elsevier
225 Wyman Street, Waltham, MA 02451, USA
The Boulevard, Langford Lane, Kidlington, Oxford, OX5 1 GB, UK

Notices
Knowledge and best practice in this field are constantly changing. As new research and experience broaden our understanding, changes in research methods or professional practices, may become necessary.

Practitioners and researchers must always rely on their own experience and knowledge in evaluating and using any information or methods described herein. In using such information or methods they should be mindful of their own safety and the safety of others, including parties for whom they have a professional responsibility.

To the fullest extent of the law, neither the Publisher nor the authors, contributors, or editors, assume any liability for any injury and/or damage to persons or property as a matter of products liability, negligence or otherwise, or from any use or operation of any methods, products, instructions, or ideas contained in the material herein.

Library of Congress Cataloging-in-Publication Data
Sennewald, Charles A., 1931-
  From the files of a security expert witness / Charles A. Sennewald.
      pages cm
  Includes bibliographical references and index.
  ISBN 978-0-12-411625-2 (alk. paper)
  1. Private security services—Law and legislation—United States. 2. Security consultants—Legal status, laws, etc.—United States. 3. Evidence, Expert—United States. I. Title.
  KF5399.5.P7S46 2013
  347.73'67—dc23   2013009978

British Library Cataloguing-in-Publication Data
A catalogue record for this book is available from the British Library

For information on all Butterworth–Heinemann publications
visit our website at http://store.elsevier.com

DEDICATION

Dedicated to IHS

"...so help me God."

CONTENTS

ACKNOWLEDGMENTS

I gratefully acknowledge the publishing professionals Pam Chester, M. J. Peluso, Shirley Decker-Lucke, and Amber Hodge who collectively exercised the magic of turning my memories into print. I warmly acknowledge my wife and best friend, Connie, whose early belief in this work and continued encouragement inspired me to stay the course and complete the manuscript.

INTRODUCTION

Because we are a society of laws, laws influence everything we do, from buying a home and engaging in business to how we drive and how we conduct ourselves with others. Failure to comply with the law invariably leads to some appropriate resolution in the courts, the judicial system, which ensures compliance through confinement, fines, or civil court awards of compensation.

Most court resolutions occur as a result of a trial that weighs the facts, sorts through conflicting input, and arrives at, hopefully, a fair and impartial decision. That process requires the presence of witnesses whose testimony illuminates the historical event being examined. No witnesses, no trial. Therefore, witnesses are the life blood of the court trial, irrespective of the nature of the contest.

There are two kinds of witnesses: fact witnesses and expert witnesses. Fact witnesses may only testify to what they actually saw, heard, felt, or smelled. Such witnesses are restricted from testifying about any opinions they may have formed as a result of what they learned through their own senses. Expert witnesses, on the other hand, may express opinions based on their in-depth examination of the event through the lens of their unique experience, education, and profession.

Experts in criminal trials include specialists in subjects such as DNA, fingerprint identification, blood and liquid splattering patterns, firearms identification, explosives, and cause of death. Experts who appear in civil trials represent an incredibly vast range of disciplines, from construction failures, to airplane crashes, to beer keg explosions, to auto tire failures, all of which cause injuries. It would take an entire chapter to list the various expert witness specialties which exist in our society. Hence, the opinions of all experts are based on their unique and specialized expertise, as approved by the court.

This book focuses on my role as a security expert witness and my involvement in a collection of actual civil lawsuits driven by criminal acts. The second trial of O. J. Simpson in Los Angeles, CA, is a prime example of a crime litigated in the civil court. A criminal trial determines if a defendant is guilty of a crime (a public offense), and a civil trial determines if a defendant is guilty of a tort (a civil wrong). The burden of proof is higher in a criminal prosecution—that is, "beyond a reasonable doubt"—and lesser for finding against a defendant in a civil proceeding—"a preponderance of evidence." In the cases of O. J. Simpson, he was found not guilty in the criminal trial, but was found responsible for the deaths in the civil court proceeding.

The "beyond a reasonable doubt" test requires unanimous agreement of all jurors, whereas only a majority of jurors in a civil trial are required to meet the test of "a preponderance of evidence." Many crimes find their way into civil court, irrespective of the criminal trial's outcome. However, there's another significant difference between a civil trial and criminal proceedings. For example, if a woman is kidnapped from a parking lot and is eventually brutalized, the only defendant in the criminal system is the perpetrator of the crime. In civil court, for the very same crime, the defendants invariably include not only the perpetrator of the crime, but the owners or managers of the parking lot, the security firm charged with patrolling the lot, and, perhaps, the maintenance company responsible for ensuring the lights in the lot were all properly working. The typical issues in these types of cases are whether the crime was a foreseeable event and did the defendants take reasonable steps to provide a safe parking environment for invitees on their property. The bottom line: the thrust of the civil litigation in this case is to determine if the defendant did wrong or failed to do right and, therefore, were part of the causation of the damage done to the woman who was the crime victim.

Readers of the various scenarios in this book will follow the expert witness process of evaluating and determining the action, be it the plaintiff's theory of liability or the defendant's theory of defense, and observe my determination if my client's (or prospective client's) position/theory is meritorious. Both sides retain the best expert they can find and often the jury (or the court) will be persuaded, in some measure, by one of the opposing expert's opinions.

Therefore, the process, as stated earlier, is ideal because the court and the jurors have the benefit of shared expert insight and wisdom that clarify areas that are otherwise outside the range of the average person's understanding.

This all comes down to the process of litigation. Regrettably, there are those in this judicial arena who skate on the thin ice of integrity an elusive quality. That's to say some attorneys will undertake lawsuits that they know, or should know, really lack merit, and there are so-called "expert witnesses" who undertake assignments that they are not qualified for (i.e., they exaggerate or otherwise misrepresent their professional credentials).

The legal community has a duty to purge their ranks of renegade lawyers and be more and ever diligent in vetting the qualifications of their experts.

This book was written to provide readers with a fresh and insightful journey through some very brutal crimes, descriptions of how and why they are committed, clarifications of the process or methodology of a true expert in forming opinions, and the litigious process thereafter, with its inevitable consequences.

Every chapter deals with a different criminal incident or incidents, and only the names of the defendants and plaintiffs, as well as the location of the events, have been changed to ensure their anonymity.

CHAPTER *1*

Greene v. Holy Spirit Hospital

Contents

WHAT HAPPENED?

A young female employee of Holy Spirit Hospital was abducted from the parking ramp, taken to an isolated area not far from the hospital, forcibly raped, and, during the rape, strangled to death and her body abandoned.

WHO WAS BEING SUED, AND WHY?

The hospital was being sued by the victim's surviving family members. The lawsuit alleged the hospital's security program was negligent and inadequate.

WHO WAS INVOLVED?

- Vivian Greene, a 21-year-old nurse's assistant, who typically worked the day shift at Holy Spirit Hospital.
- Danny Greene, a 23-year-old furniture salesman who married Vivian two weeks prior to the murder.
- Betty Rankowski, the mother of the victim, who was also a nurse's assistant at Holy Spirit Hospital and worked the day shift.
- Jo Rankowski, the victim's 12-year-old sister.
- Robert Corley, a 26-year-old newly released inmate from the state prison given an early release by the governor because of an act of heroism.

- James T. Trenton, the state governor who authorized the early and unexpected release of Robert Corley.
- Mr. and Mrs. McGrath, the resident managers of the state's halfway house for released inmates.
- Tom Case, the director of security at Holy Spirit Hospital.

WHEN DID IT HAPPEN?

On a Thursday evening in early December around 9:00 p.m.

HOW DID IT HAPPEN?

With no scheduled releases of inmates for the next two weeks, the McGraths planned on a well-earned vacation away from the residence and job as overseers of the state's halfway house—that is, the strategy of temporarily housing and supervising newly released inmates in their transition back into society.

A week before the tragic crime, a riot in one of the prison's cellblocks broke out. In the following pandemonium, inmate Robert Corley personally pulled a guard into a safe location, preventing any injury to the man, and in so doing incurred some risk to himself. This act of heroism came to the attention of Governor James Trenton who expressed his gratitude by authorizing an early release for Robert.

The unexpected release caught the McGraths off-guard. Should they cancel their vacation? After meeting and talking with Robert they felt comfortable with letting him stay alone in the halfway house in their absence. He understood the rules, which included no alcohol or drugs. They left Tuesday.

The week prior to the fateful event, the victim's mother, Betty Rankowski, agreed to work a double shift on the next Thursday so a coworker could attend a party. It was a special favor for a friend. That meant that her daughter Vivian would have to drive home alone after the day shift. Because the newlyweds were struggling financially, they ate at Betty's each evening, then went home in Danny Greene's car to their small apartment. Each morning Danny would drop off Vivian at Betty's house and the two nurses' aides would drive to work together. At the end of the day they all gathered at Betty's and had supper together.

On Wednesday, Robert, now enjoying his freedom and staying in the halfway house, borrowed a friend's car and, with another ex-con, obtained marijuana, smoked it, and started partying with two female acquaintances. The partying included sex, along with smoking marijuana and consuming whisky, lasting into midday Thursday. During the partying, Robert's friend injured his hand, either striking someone or something, and the two drove to Holy Spirit Hospital for emergency treatment of the injury.

Nothing eventful occurred during that daytime visit, other than Robert watching the staff.

That same Thursday Vivian and Betty drove to the hospital together in Betty's car, reporting for work on the day shift. There was no evidence Robert saw either of them or they saw Robert.

At the end of the shift, Betty stayed at the hospital for the second shift and Vivian drove to her mother's home where she met Danny and her little sister, Jo. The three ate while watching television. Following dinner, Vivian planned to drive her mother's car back to the hospital's parking ramp, followed by Danny. She would park on the third level, lock the car, walk across the skywalk into the hospital, and return the car keys to her mother. She would then return across the skywalk to the elevators in the parking structure and descend to the street level where Danny would be waiting at the curb.

Sometime right after Vivian drove out of that parking structure, Robert drove in, alone, and parked the car on the third level. It was a cold evening with a light dusting of snow. Not many cars were parked in the ramp and there was no parking attendant. The only planned oversight of the ramp was the periodic patrols of a hospital security officer. Robert sat in his vehicle with the driver's door open, legs out, drinking whiskey, smoking, and listening to country music. One witness later testified she observed him and just assumed he was waiting for someone, although it struck her as odd because it was so cold and damp in the concrete structure and the young man didn't appear to be dressed warmly enough. Another witness had a similar reaction.

Following supper and a couple television programs, Danny and Vivian cleaned the kitchen and prepared to return Betty's car and go home. Vivian asked her sister if she would like to go with her. Jo said she'd rather watch television so they left her behind. Danny followed his wife and, as they approached the entrance to the hospital's parking ramp, Danny parked parallel to the curb and watched his wife drive into the ramp's entrance. He sat there with his motor running, headlights on, music play-ing, with the wipers moving slowly, whisking away the powdery snow-flakes. He expected to wait for her perhaps 10 minutes at the most.

Robert, still sitting in his car (the only car in that area) watched Vivian pull into a space close to him, get out of her car, and start toward the sky-walk. He stood up, pretending he was about to walk into the skywalk, and, as she passed near him, he reached out and grabbed her arm. She was star-tled and speechless. He pulled her to his car telling her he wouldn't hurt her if she didn't scream and complied with his instructions. She begged him not to hurt her, that she would do as he said, and that if it was drugs he wanted, she could get some because she worked in the hospital. He forced her into the passenger side of the car and told her he'd kill her if she screamed. She was anxious not to alarm him or trigger him into acting violently and acquiesced to each command. He told her to get down on the floorboard with her head under the glove box so she couldn't be seen, and drove slowly out of the ramp. When he reached the exit and the street there was a car to his left with its headlights on. He made a left turn in front of the car and proceeded away with her still crouching on the floor.

Danny watched a car slowly exit the ramp. His headlights fully illumi-nated the old Chevrolet and the young man at the wheel. There was abso-lutely nothing suspicious about this, but Danny had an unexplainable eerie feeling and was curious as to why the man turned left since it would only lead, some blocks down the street, to the railroad yards and a dead-end. Not four minutes had elapsed since Vivian drove into the ramp.

A couple minutes later, the same old car approached Danny from his rear. Danny was right about the driver turning in the wrong direction. As the car slowly passed him again, the same spooky feeling returned. He did not have a reason for this chilling feeling but did consciously make a men-tal note of the car's license plate.

Robert drove with his victim still crouched on the floor to a remote location by the river and, while parked there, raped the young bride. In the process of raping the woman, he decided to choke her to death to feel any contractions that might occur during the process.

When he finished, he dumped her nude body in the weeds along the roadside and returned to the halfway house.

After waiting 15 minutes for Vivian, Danny became impatient and drove onto the ramp to see what was keeping her. On the third level he spotted Betty's car. It was locked. He walked over the skywalk and into the hospi-tal and found his mother-in-law and asked where Vivian was. Betty said she hadn't seen Vivian. They conducted a search of the hospital. Security was asked to assist and one of the two officers joined in the search. It was finally concluded Vivian wasn't in the hospital, wasn't in the car, and wasn't at Betty's house. No one answered the phone in the Greene's apartment, so the police were summoned to the hospital. During the on-scene investigation Danny informed the police of his observation of the old Chevrolet, described it and the driver, and repeated the license number he had memorized.

The next morning Vivian's body was found by a passerby.

The police ran the license number through the department of motor vehicles but it didn't match up with the suspect vehicle or its registered location in the state. The description of the vehicle, including the "bad" license plate number, was broadcast to all police agencies in the state. A short time later that morning a police officer on routine patrol spotted a car parked on the side of the halfway house fitting the description in the broadcast. The license plate bore the numbers provided by Danny except he had inadvertently transposed two numbers. Betty's car keys were on the passenger's side floorboard.

A groggy and hungover Robert was taken into custody and shortly thereafter confessed to the crime.

ASSESSMENT OF THE SECURITY PROGRAM

Tom Case, a retired local city police officer, was the hospital's director of security. He reported to the chief maintenance engineer. This was a classic mistake in organizational design because security had no mid-management voice in such matters as budgeting. Security requests by the director of security would be subject to the chief engineer's priorities. This organizational design typically has the head of housekeeping and janitorial services on par with security.

Case had made frequent requests for additional security personnel, citing problems at this multistory, 400-bed hospital campus, and the inability of his small staff to cover the facility that spread over several city blocks. Those requests were ignored. The budget didn't allow for a security supervisor for each shift. The only supervisor was the director himself. Indeed, his staff was comprised of off-duty police officers so the administration wouldn't have to pay employee benefits. Most security experts agree off-duty police officers don't make the best security officers for a number of reasons, including that their focus, identity, and loyalty is with their police service and departments.

Payroll and time-keeping records disclosed two security officers were on duty at the time of the abduction. One was assisting a maintenance man in relocating television sets in patients' rooms and the other was temporarily serving as receptionist during the evening hours. Because activity logs, which typically reflect what officers do on a given shift, weren't required, there was no audit trail to identify who patrolled outside and when. Both officers testified they conducted exterior patrols but could offer no specifics. Both claimed they patrolled the parking ramp but neither recalled seeing Robert. It was not possible for a patrolling officer in the ramp to not see Robert because he was parked in the very path leading to and from the skywalk and, as noted earlier, was engaged in obvious, unusual, and conspicuous conduct. The only logical conclusion I (or anyone) could make is the officers did not patrol the parking ramp, as required.

Hospital visitors saw Robert, but not security. Witnesses established Robert was in the parking ramp for two hours. And Robert, during his interrogation of the event by police detectives, stated he didn't see security officers. It's reasonable to assume he would have left the ramp had he seen such a patrol. Further, the security department didn't have a dedicated patrol vehicle so they were obliged to go out and walk around the campus in the snow. Human nature, as it is, tends to take routes of ease and least resistance and avoid, if possible, unpleasant (and seemingly unimportant) tasks. I was of the opinion the security officers failed to patrol that ramp on an hourly basis, as required.

The news of what happened to Vivian spread like wildfire throughout the hospital, and Case was overheard saying, "I told them this would happen, I just don't have the staff."

Interestingly, because of a rape of a nurse at the other hospital in town a couple years prior, the hospital established a policy requiring a security officer to escort any employee or visitor out to his or her vehicle, upon request. There was no such security for those entering the facility from a parking area.

ASSESSMENT OF CRIME STATISTICS IN THE COMMUNITY

City crime statistics were on average with comparable cities in that part of the United States. That is, the nature and frequency of part-one crimes (i.e., murder, rape, aggravated assault, robbery, burglary, auto theft, and larceny) were comparable with other cities of similar size, nothing remarkable. In terms of any well-publicized crimes in recent history (the preceding three years), the other hospital in the city did experience a violent incident of rape of a nurse. Following that violent crime there was a clamor for more and better lighting at that hospital and nurses and staff at Holy Spirit took up the same cause. Lighting and the level of illumination at Holy Spirit wasn't an issue in the Greene matter.

The distribution of crime within a city is usually divided into geographical districts or beats. For example, in some communities there's an old and seedy downtown area with noisy and grubby cocktail lounges and bars. The area might be six blocks long and six blocks wide. That area is a beat or "reporting district"—let's identify it as beat 10. Two miles away is a new residential housing district of the same geographical size, beat 22. Invariably more crimes occurred in beat 10 (e.g., 175 crimes) than in beat 22 (e.g., 50 crimes). So police beats or reporting districts will be classified as a high-crime area, an average crime area, or a low-crime area depending on the number of criminal incidents that occurred inside that area. Holy Spirit Hospital was located in a reporting district with an average amount of crime—that is, not high and not low.

As for the hospital campus itself, various crimes occurred, as reported to the police. In the three years prior to the Greene murder the only crimes against persons or a sex-related incident included a parking lot robbery of a visitor, an attempted sexual assault on a female staff member, and an indecent exposure to a visitor. Various other crimes, such as thefts, vandalism, intoxicated persons creating disturbances, etc. were ongoing and common to this kind of environment and not remarkable.

The parking ramp from which Vivian was abducted had more reported problems than the rest of the campus. Whereas the immediate area of the abduction was adequately illuminated (apparently because it was at the entrance to the skywalk) the rest of this multistory parking ramp was more dimly lit. A history of vandalism, breaking of lighting fixtures, graffiti, theft from vehicles, theft of vehicles, fighting, and gathering of youths who used the isolated upper floors for drinking and partying including smoking of marijuana, indicated it was a magnet for problems, as well as not properly policed or supervised.

THE RESULTS OF MY ASSESSMENT

My opinion, after an exhaustive review of all available information, as well as a personal inspection of the facility, was as follows:

1. The hospital administration knew they had ongoing problems, particularly on the parking ramp.
2. Despite being aware of the problems, management failed to take reasonable steps to improve its security program.

3. The security program was below the standard of care and inadequate for the task at hand.

4. The crime against Vivian Greene was not specifically foreseeable, however, a serious crime occurring on that ramp was foreseeable, in view of the totality of circumstances.

The state district court judge disagreed and threw out the case (i.e., dismissed it) in response to the defendants' motion for summary judgment—that is, the cause of action (the complaint) lacked merit and was not worthy of a trial.

The plaintiff law firm appealed the decision to the state supreme court, of which the justices decided the case was worthy of a hearing. The district court's ruling was overturned and the matter was remanded back to the district court for trial. Such decisions are called "case law."

The trial was the talk of the town. Local television coverage was the top of the evening news each day as the trial progressed. I had testified in numerous civil court trials prior to this matter and rarely do I see more than 20 spectators present in the courtroom. In this trial there was standing-room only. It was a matter of high drama and grave concern to the community. Here was an important Catholic hospital, practically an icon in the community, being sued. There were Catholics on the jury. Everyone knew the governor had released Robert. Everyone knew the McGraths had left Robert unsupervised. Everyone knew local off-duty policemen provided security for the hospital. This violent crime seemed to have touched everyone. Would the hospital win or lose this lawsuit?

I was called to the stand as the plaintiffs' attorneys neared the end of their case. I testified as to my opinions. When cross-examined by the defense counsel, one of his first questions was, "Mr. Sennewald, how much are you being paid for your testimony?" My response, "I'm not paid for my testimony. No one can buy my testimony. I'm compensated for my time, and I charge an hourly fee." He asked, "Well then, sir, what is your hourly fee?" knowing full well what my fee was because he had to pay for my deposition testimony some months earlier. When I answered there was an audible gasp throughout the entire court room. No one had ever heard of such a high hourly rate in this small city (unless they had the unfortunate experience of paying a top lawyer's fees, which most people never do). Attorney fees and expert witness fees are relatively comparable.

Asking experts about their fees in front of a jury is a subtle strategy aimed at alienating the expert from one or more jurors who might resent someone charging such high fees. Most people automatically calculate hourly fees into 40 hours a week. Experts don't work 40 hours a week on a regular basis.

Perhaps the heart of my testimony in this matter was reflected in the following exchange with the defense counsel when he asked, "Mr. Sennewald, are you suggesting to the good people of this small community that we need the same kind of security in our hospital as you'll find in hospitals in Los Angeles?" My reply:

> Yes. Every hospital must have security and the people of this community who work and visit your hospital are deserving of the same level of protection as those who work at and visit hospitals in Los Angeles. And I might add, sir, I note your community needs and has a police department, just like the people of Los Angeles need and have a police department. Crime happens everywhere.

The jury found for the plaintiffs, awarding them over a half million dollars, a remarkable award for that period of time in that part of the country.

POSTSCRIPT

This tragic event weighed heavily on various people, as follows:

Betty felt a sense of guilt for working the double shift because she would not have lost her daughter had she refused that request. Working that shift was really driven by a form of greed—that is, her friend would owe her a day off in the future.

Danny felt guilty for not following Vivian up to the third floor of the ramp. His presence would have deterred the attack, and his wife would still be alive. There really was no excuse or good reason for him *not* to have followed her up.

Jo felt a sense of guilt for not accompanying her sister because she wanted to be a "couch potato" and watch television. Had she been in the car with her sister, Vivian would still be alive.

Governor Trenton felt he was in some measure to blame for his hasty decision to cause the early and unscheduled release of a known criminal. Had he followed the normal procedures, Vivian would still be alive.

The McGraths felt guilty for taking their Florida vacation and leaving Robert unsupervised. Had they discharged their responsibility to supervise and assist newly released inmates, Vivian would still be alive.

Case felt some culpability, as well as frustration, that such a heinous crime occurred on "his watch." Had he been more persistent in convincing the hospital a supervisor was needed for every shift and had he done his job effectively, he would have a sufficient, properly trained, and supervised staff that could have prevented the conditions that lead to Vivian's death.

Following this tragedy, the security department's budget was increased and its level of professionalism rose, more in keeping with the excellent reputation of the hospital itself.

Everyone recognizes there are no guarantees when it comes to human behavior and crime, but it's unlikely such an event will occur at Holy Spirit Hospital again.

CHAPTER 2

Yamamoto v. Harbor View Homeowners' Association

Contents

WHAT HAPPENED?

A young, single woman was found lying dead on the floor of her 14th-story apartment in a secured condominium complex. She had been injured in a scuffle and suffocated with a pillow.

WHO WAS BEING SUED, AND WHY?

The Harbor View Homeowners' Association was the named defendant. They were being sued on the grounds their security officers were negligent in allowing the murderer, the victim's former boyfriend, access to the secured complex and her apartment.

WHO WAS INVOLVED?

- Annie Yamamoto, condominium resident and victim of the homicide.
- Sonny Fatau, Annie's former boyfriend and admitted assailant.
- Fred Miller, condominium security officer assigned to the graveyard shift.
- Charlie Wong, condominium security officer assigned to the graveyard shift.
- Barbara Andrews, Annie's friend and coworker who discovered the body.

WHEN DID IT HAPPEN?

July 3 at approximately 2:45 a.m.

HOW DID IT HAPPEN?

Unit 1404 had a magnificent view of the harbor. The unit was owned by a Japanese national who was friends of the Yamamoto family. He had little reason to travel to the United States anymore and allowed Annie Yamamoto to live in his stateside condo. Annie had a challenging job in the fishing industry. She and two of her coworkers, Sonny Fatau and Barbara Andrews, socialized both on and off the job. As time passed, Annie and Sonny's friendship developed into a romantic affair.

Annie invited Sonny to move his personal effects into unit 1404, and the two set up house together. Every resident had an electronic access card that unlocked the lobby doors and allowed access to the elevator banks. Without the card, one could not enter the lobby. Guests, visitors, and vendors were required to use a phone mounted on the exterior wall. Using a resident directory posted on the wall next to the phone, the visitor could call the desired apartment, and the resident from his or her apartment could remotely release the lock to allow entry (i.e., "buzz them in").

Sonny wasn't issued an access card because he wasn't an owner. He could have been issued a card, but Annie reasoned that there was no reason for him to have one. After all, they left each morning for work together, returned home at the end of the day together, went out at night together, and so on. Sonny rarely had occasion during the two months he lived there to come or go alone. And if he did, he'd call Annie from the visitor's phone and she'd release the lobby door lock from her apartment. All the security officers knew Annie before the relationship, and subsequently mentally identified Sonny as Annie's live-in boyfriend.

After a couple of months the romance cooled and Annie came to the conclusion the relationship was over. She asked Sonny to move his things out of her apartment. He begged her to think it over, but she was adamant. It was Saturday morning, July 1. Sonny made three trips through the lobby, past security officers, during his moving, and was readmitted each time by using the outside phone and having her remotely release the lock on the door.

After getting settled back in his old room at his parent's home, he phoned Annie, but each time she would hang up on him. Although she was happy the relationship was over, he was crushed by the turn of events and wanted to find some way to reestablish the affair. That Saturday evening he visited all the clubs and bars they typically spent time in, hoping to find her and engage her in a reasonable discussion that surely would end up bringing them back together. He couldn't find her that night.

In a phone conversation with a friend the following day, Sonny agonized over his inability to get Annie to talk with him or find her. His friend told him several of their regular group, including Annie, would be at the Mariner's Club around 10:00 p.m. that night.

Sonny arrived at the Mariner's Club at 9:30 p.m., ordered a drink, and waited for Annie to arrive. However, 10:00 p.m. came and went with no group and no Annie. Another friend wandered in; when questioned, he said he had seen everyone, including Annie, at the TropiGal Club. Sonny settled up with the bartender and walked the bayfront to the next nightclub. Inside it was smoky and dark as music roared on this typically crowded Sunday night. Sonny easily worked his way to the bar, given his substantial frame. With drink in hand, he moved among the partygoers until he spotted Annie. She had already been alerted to the fact he was looking for her, she so steeled herself for a confrontation. When they came face-to-face she again told him it was over and he needed to get out of her life. He tried to convince her it wasn't necessarily over. In her view he was becoming a real nuisance who wouldn't let go, so she excused herself to go to the restroom, gathered a couple friends, and slipped out the side door. He ordered another drink and maintained a watch on the ladies' restroom until he realized he must have missed her and she must have gone home.

Sonny, now somewhat under the influence of alcohol, decided he would go to the condo and try again to discuss their relationship. He walked the bayfront, arriving at the lobby doors about 1:30 a.m. It was now early Monday morning and the streets were empty. The lobby was brightly illuminated, and the uniformed security officer, Fred Miller, was seated at a desk with his back against the wall, facing the glass doors. Miller watched Sonny go to the visitor phone and could tell he was calling a resident.

Sonny dialed unit 1404 and let the phone ring at least 20 times. No answer. He hung up the phone and went to the double glass doors and waved the security officer to the doors. The officer recognized Sonny as Annie's boyfriend, but didn't know Sonny had been evicted.

Miller walked to the door, opened it, and asked Sonny what he wanted. "She won't answer," he said. The officer then instructed him to try calling again. Sonny returned to the wall phone and redialed. Miller allowed the door to fully close and it was again in a locked mode, but he stood near the door and continued to watch Sonny on the phone. As the officer watched, he saw Sonny in the process of hanging up just as the electric latch of the door buzzed open. Sonny moved toward the unlocked door, but just as he was about to push the door open, the buzzing latch reset and the door was again locked. The security officer was of the belief Sonny had indeed made contact with his roommate and the lock was opened from the unit, but Sonny was too slow to make the door in time. So Miller unlocked the door and allowed him in. Sonny indeed had not talked to her on the phone but assumed (because the door had inexplicably been remotely opened) she had realized he still wanted to talk and decided to let him in.

He took elevator #1 and ascended to the 14th floor. He knocked on the door of unit 1404 and called her name numerous times but there was no answer. While Sonny was on the 14th floor, the security officers made their scheduled post changes and rotated to different locations within the complex. Miller, who had been in the north lobby, was now replaced by Officer Charlie Wong, who took up his position at the desk. Typically, when an officer is relieved he advises the new person of any conditions or events that may be of importance. Miller had nothing unusual to report to the new officer.

Frustrated over Annie's refusal to open the door, Sonny returned to the lobby and approached Wong, who recognized Sonny. Sonny complained that Annie was being stubborn and wouldn't let him in and he asked Wong to use his key to let him in. Wong responded, "You know I can't do that. If she won't let you in, then you're out of luck. It's against policy for me to open any apartment without the specific authorization of the resident and you're not listed here in the directory as a resident." Sonny said he'd go back up and try again. Sonny, clearly, believed she had left the TropiGal Club, returned directly home, and was in the unit. This belief was reinforced with the complex door's latch being remotely unlocked.

Wong watched Sonny while he rode up in elevator #1 on his closed-circuit television monitor. Every elevator cab was monitored. While casually watching Sonny, he noticed a taxi pull under the porte-cochere and saw a young woman exit, pay the driver, and approach the lobby doors. It was Annie. She used her access card, entered the lobby, said "Hi" to Wong, entered elevator #2, and ascended to the 14th floor.

Sonny was again in the process of knocking on the door when he heard an elevator open. He turned in that direction and around the corner came Annie, who, shocked at his presence, exclaimed, "What the hell are you doing here?" Sonny tried to explain he thought she had let him in and all he wanted to do was have a few minutes to talk about their breakup. "Please," he pleaded. In exasperation she said okay, but insisted their visit must be brief because of the late hour.

Entry into the unit commences with a long narrow hallway opening into the living room. They sat down across from one another. Both had been drinking, and their voices were somewhat raised. The discussion about why she wanted to end the relationship deteriorated into an argument. The arguing brought them both to their feet. Suddenly, Annie forcefully slapped Sonny in the face. Infuriated by being struck, Sonny struck her back. They again exchanged blows, several times, each one more forcibly delivered. Both grappled with one another, and they fell to the floor, with her screaming. Several little tables, including the one on which her purse had been placed, and a lamp were knocked over. Sonny, significantly larger than Annie, grabbed a pillow and pushed it into her face and smothered her screams. Eventually she relaxed. He released the pillow and observed that she was now unconscious. Bleeding and distraught, he left her on the floor, returned to the elevators, and rode elevator #2 down to the lobby. Officer Wong watched him on the monitor as he descended. Nothing unusual was noted. The time on the videotape reflected 3:03 a.m. Sonny left the building by the east door and walked home.

Upon arriving at home he called her apartment but there was no answer. He went to bed. Several hours later, Sonny called her apartment again because she didn't show up at the office. Barbara came by and asked where Annie was. Sonny said he didn't know. That day he called the apartment several times, with no answer. Sonny assumed she didn't feel well after their fight and wasn't answering her phone.

The next day was a holiday and the company's annual picnic, a big event. Annie didn't show up, which started to cause Sonny some alarm. Barbara was mystified because she couldn't reach Annie either. Her inability to contact Annie turned to alarm. When Annie failed to report for work on the morning of July 5, Barbara went to Harbor View and, again, after no answer from the unit, asked to speak to the manager on duty at the desk. Barbara explained Annie hadn't been seen since Sunday night and something must be wrong. Reluctantly, the manger used a passkey and the two entered unit 1404. The manager led the way down the narrow hallway and was the first to enter the living room. He immediately said, "Stay back. Don't look in here," but Barbara pushed past the manager, then threw her hands to her mouth and moaned when she saw the body of her friend on the floor in the disheveled living room, obviously dead. The two, both mortified, quietly backed out and called the police.

The next day, following the detective's investigation, which included interviewing the security officers who were on duty and viewing the security camera videotapes, Sonny was taken into police custody. He confessed to the crime, although he claimed it was not intentional and thought she had simply passed out from too much drinking and too much fighting.

ASSESSMENT OF THE PLAINTIFF'S THEORY

This was a straightforward civil complaint that, but for the security officer's act of allowing Sonny into the building, there would have been no murder. The plaintiff's position was the officer's negligence was the proximate cause of the crime. The essence of the lawsuit centered on one question: Was the act of opening the door and letting Sonny in negligent or not?

Other issues, such as whether or not this was a foreseeable act because of the history of crime in the complex, did not come into play in this case. Why not? Because this murder would have been considered a crime of domestic violence or a crime involving parties who were acquainted. Had the crime not been solved or had the death of Annie been a mysterious event with the belief or possibility the perpetrator was a stranger who had unlawfully gained entrance into the complex and randomly preyed on a hapless victim, then the issue could have been classified as a "premises liability" case, which includes the theory the property was dangerous, crimes of violence were foreseeable, and the security procedures failed to make the property safe.

The civil lawsuit always follows the criminal matter, like in the O. J. Simpson murder case. Simpson was prosecuted for a crime (a public offense) and was found not guilty in the criminal courts, because the jury must unanimously agree the suspect is guilty of the offense beyond a reasonable doubt. Subsequently, he was prosecuted by the plaintiffs in the civil court for a tort (a civil wrong) and was convicted for his commission of an injury (the murder). The burden of proof in civil court is remarkably less than in criminal court: it only requires a preponderance of evidence to find one culpable.

This action against the Harbor View Condominiums followed the criminal action against Sonny, and the plaintiffs and their legal counsel had the benefit of all the information that was obtained by the police, which was the platform or resource of information for their case. Yes, they sued Sonny as well, even though he was in prison. However, the Harbor View Homeowners' Association was the real target (in reality, their insurance company had the real "deep pockets"). I was retained by the law firm defending the Harbor View Homeowners' Association.

When the police arrived at the scene on the morning of July 5 they had to start with a blank page. They had no information other than the name of the victim and the apparent cause of death. They had no idea if this was an act of domestic violence or a predatory crime.

Accordingly, a classic and standard homicide investigation was launched, conducted by experienced homicide detectives, and all necessary steps were taken to preserve and record the crime scene. Such steps included taking numerous photographs, an evidence technician drawing the crime scene, the search for latent fingerprints (and lifting and preservation of any), and the lifting of blood stains for subsequent comparison and DNA analysis. It should be noted that the drawing of a crime scene is like looking down on the room from above. The resultant diagram clearly reflects the spatial relationship of the body to other objects in the room, including specific distances, the location of any weapon that may have been left behind, the location of blood spatter, and the location of furniture, etc. Photographs supplement the drawing.

While this focused activity on the scene was underway, the detectives concentrated their efforts on locating and interviewing witnesses. Barbara advised the investigators she and Annie went to her apartment in The Wave complex from the TropiGal Club. Annie left The Wave complex in a taxi about 2:30 a.m., presumably headed for home. The three graveyard officers who would have been on duty between midnight and 8:00 a.m., including Officers Miller and Wong, were called in. Their recollection of the events and the retrieval and review of the videotapes clearly identified Sonny was a possible suspect.

Sonny was taken into custody as he left work that afternoon. He was escorted to his home where the clothing he was wearing Sunday night was seized for crime lab analysis.

At the police station, Sonny admitted his confrontation with Annie, claiming he was provoked into violence and his only intention was to subdue her. He appeared contrite. His subsequent detailed confession was recorded. Indeed, the scenario of events, as outlined in this chapter, is almost wholly Sonny's version of what transpired, and the bulk of material that was available for my review and analysis of the event.

The entire police file, usually a voluminous package, is referred to in the police profession as a "Murder Book." In my task as forensic consultant and expert for the defense, I was obliged to read and absorb the contents of this material.

Sonny was indicted for murder. Following the preliminary hearing, he waived his right to trial, pled to a lesser offense, and was sentenced to the state penitentiary for 25 years.

ASSESSMENT OF THE SECURITY OFFICERS' CONDUCT

Review of the Harbor View Condominium's policies and procedures, examination of the security officers' job descriptions, and interviews with key employees and managers of the complex revealed that security officers were not directly involved in the electronic access control program. Access cards were issued and controlled by management, not security. That was also true with the replacement of lost cards. Put another way, security officers did not control access to the complex. They did, however, augment the controls during nonbusiness hours (5:00 p.m. to 7:00 a.m.) by their assigned presence in the front lobby. For example, if a resident lost his or her card and couldn't get in, the security officer could allow that individual passage if that resident's identity and ownership of a unit was confirmed. There was an up-to-date directory of residents, to which the officer could refer. The officer's visible presence in the lobby also served as a deterrent to those who might want to follow a resident in while the door was unlocked, referred to as *tailgating*.

The two specific issues centered on Officers Miller and Wong:

- The plaintiff maintained, as did their security expert, Miller acted negligently when he opened the locked door and allowed Sonny to enter the lobby.
- I, on the other hand, opined that Miller's opening the door, in view of the circumstances, was a reasonable act. Indeed, I held the position that if he had refused to open the door, under those very circumstances, his conduct would have been unreasonable.

What were those circumstances?

1. Miller recognized Sonny as a resident (as opposed to a stranger) or at least a temporary resident, and prudently did not allow Sonny to enter when told the resident wouldn't answer the phone and release the lock. Miller sent him back to the phone to try again.
2. Miller stood there and oversaw Sonny's second attempt to contact the resident.

3. Miller stood at the door and heard and saw the latch being released as Sonny was hanging up the phone. The only reasonable conclusion one could draw from the unfolding sequence of events was the tenant had indeed activated the release. The only people on the scene were Miller and Sonny. The release of the latch obviously wasn't for some other guest because there was no other guest. Although it's an inexplicable event, in hindsight, that release of the latch at that very moment in time could only be interpreted by the security officer as the authorization by the tenant to allow Sonny in.

The plaintiff and their security expert witness took the position that Wong knew Sonny was having a problem getting the resident to open the door to her apartment. Wong also knew Sonny exited the elevator on the 14th floor and was obviously up there. With that knowledge Wong then saw the resident, Annie, enter the lobby. The plaintiff's contention was it was negligent on Wong's part not to warn her that her boyfriend was up there. Had he warned her, she would not, in all likelihood, have gone up, and would be alive.

That contention was probably true. Had Annie known Sonny was standing at her door she probably would have avoided another confrontation and asked the officers to remove him, or call the police to remove him.

But the real issue was: Did Wong have a duty to warn her? Was he required or obliged to warn her? On the surface it would appear that indeed he should have. But a careful reflection on the events, in my view, was why would he warn her? He had no duty to warn because:

1. He recognized Sonny as the live-in boyfriend of a resident.
2. He had no information that Sonny had been unofficially evicted by the resident.
3. He would rightfully assume, by virtue of Sonny's presence in the lobby, he had an access card to the complex and was at least entitled to be there.
4. He rightfully and prudently refused to let Sonny into the unit because he properly confirmed in the directory of residents that Sonny was not a registered resident.
5. The confusion of who was where regarding two people who live together doesn't require a security officer to sort things out if there's no apparent problem. Sonny only told Wong Annie was being stubborn. There was nothing odious or suspicious about Sonny's behavior. Neither of the two appeared angry.

6. To see Annie now enter only suggested to the officer that the confusion was over, the two were coming together, and the two would most likely retire for the night because it was late.

I testified to all the above when my deposition was taken a couple months prior to the trial.

PRETRIAL MEETING AND TRIAL

It's a common practice in defense firms for an associate attorney to work with the expert. If the matter doesn't settle and it ends up in trial, the trial lawyer for whom the associate works surfaces and wants to personally meet the expert and review the expected testimony.

I was asked to fly in the day before my appearance in court and meet Hugh Sobinsky, the attorney actually trying the case. The meeting was late afternoon, after the court recessed for the day. The plaintiff's case had been presented to the jury in its entirety and so had the defense's case, except for me. Following my testimony, the defense would rest.

We sat in Sobinsky's office; walls covered with awards, certificates, diplomas, and lots of professional football photographs, including photos of Sobinsky, an imposing lineman in his younger days. We sat on opposite sides of his big desk, with feet propped up. He held a Dixie cup to spit in—Sobinsky was addicted to chewing tobacco. He was known far and wide for his spitting into a Dixie cup. He even did it in the courtroom. It was his signature.

Sobinsky briefed me on his assessment of the trial's progress, reciting, in bits and pieces, some of the significant testimony, especially in the plaintiff's case. He said it now came down to the plaintiff's position that the guard should never have permitted Sonny access to the building. Further, the plaintiff contended that because he was allowed in, Sonny laid in wait for Annie on the 14th floor. When she approached her door he surprised her, forced her into her unit, and, while in a rage, smothered her to death. He said the matter was now worrisome and sensed the jury was sympathetic to the plaintiff's position. I pointed out how that conflicted with Sonny's version of how she let him in. He knew that, of course, but the jury didn't like or believe Sonny.

I told Sobinsky there was evidence to refute the theory Annie was forced into her own apartment. "What evidence?" he asked, "I'm unaware of any evidence. The existence of such evidence could make a major difference in the jury's view of this case."

I informed him:

I reviewed all the information in the Murder Book. The diagram of the crime scene depicts the location of Annie's purse, where it fell by the sofa where she had been sitting at the beginning of her conversation with Sonny. The contents of the purse were inventoried by the police. Among the contents was the key to her apartment. In fact the police kept and used that very key to come and go during their investigation. That purse was a small black purse that zippered shut. The zipper had to be opened to inventory its contents.

Sobinsky was incredulous. Lawyers are not supposed to be surprised at time of trial. They hate being blindsided; that's what pre-trial discovery is all about. The plaintiff's attorney was not going to like this surprise. Obviously, if the plaintiff knew of this key they wouldn't have theorized how Sonny laid in wait and abducted her and forced her into the unit. How could I have kept this highly significant bit of information secret?

I had not kept it a secret. I wasn't asked any questions, either in my sworn deposition or in any conversations with Sobinsky's associate about how the two entered the apartment. I wasn't informed until this last minute that *lying in wait* inside the complex was a theory to buttress the complaint of the security officer allowing Sonny in and subsequently watching Annie going up in the elevator. The theory of forcible entry was not an issue when I was deposed. Had it been, I would have testified that didn't happen because, had she been surprised and forced into her own apartment, the key wouldn't have been tucked away inside a zipped-closed purse; rather it would have been in the lock, or on the floor by the door. If forcibly wrestled through the doorway and dragged down the hallway leading to the living room, Annie wouldn't have had the time to replace the key in her purse and zip it closed. This revelation shocked Sobinsky, and he knew it would be a bombshell in court in the morning.

The next day, after I raised my right hand and faced the clerk of the court who asked, "Do you swear to tell the truth, the whole truth, and nothing but the truth, so help you God?" and I answered, "I do," I testified as to my opinions about the conduct of the security officers and concluded with my opinion that Annie was not surprised, seized, and forced into her apartment. Of course, I supported it with my findings about the purse and key. "Had she been surprised during her entry the key would have remained in the lock or fallen to the floor during the struggle." I could see the face of the plaintiff's attorney turn white.

The brief cross-examination by the rattled counsel concluded with one last question: "Well, Mr. Sennewald, the murderer could have placed the key into her purse and zipped it shut, couldn't he? Isn't that possible?"

I testified, "Certainly it's possible, anything's possible, but it's unlikely."

The jury found for the defense on the basis there was no negligence.

POSTSCRIPT

I later learned that during the trial, the insurance carrier had offered the plaintiffs (Annie's family in Japan) $1,000,000 to settle. The family rejected the offer and chose to continue with the trial with the belief the jury would find for the plaintiff and award a larger amount. They ended up with nothing.

CHAPTER 3

Fiske v. Silver Mine Hotel and Casino

Contents

WHAT HAPPENED?

A gambler left the Silver Mine Hotel and Casino with over $5,000 cash in his pocket, entered his motorhome in the parking lot, and was surprised by a man who had forced his way in, then attempted to knock the owner unconscious for the purpose of robbing him. During the ensuing scuffle, the owner was shot and seriously wounded.

WHO WAS BEING SUED, AND WHY?

The Silver Mine Hotel and Casino was the named defendant in this action alleging their security department failed to provide an adequate level of protection for guests and visitors, particularly in the parking lots, and was negligent in the overall supervision and deployment of security personnel throughout the complex. It was a premises liability and negligence case, and I was retained as the plaintiff's security expert.

WHO WAS INVOLVED?

- Hank Fiske, the victim of the robbery and shooting.
- Eddie Cunningham, a local unemployed carpenter with a long history of brushes with the law, who assaulted, robbed, and shot Hank.

- Kathryn Escalante, a security officer assigned to the sports book area of the casino on the swing shift.
- Daniel Henderson, a security officer assigned to the sports book area of the casino on the swing shift.
- Shawn Carlisle, a security officer assigned to the motorized patrol of the parking lots on the swing shift.
- Don Traficanto, the director of security for the Silver Mine Hotel and Casino.

WHEN DID IT HAPPEN?

February 22 at 10:10 p.m.

HOW DID IT HAPPEN?

Hank Fiske was known as a "regular" in the casino's sports book area. Every winter for the past three years, he spent his days watching the various television monitors always tuned to a variety of sporting and athletic events, including football, basketball, thoroughbred horse racing, hockey, and boxing. Hank was a sport's "nut;" he lived for sporting and wagering on athletic events. Any contest on which one could wager on the outcome, Hank would wager. Not only was he an ardent fan, he was viewed as a "high roller" in the sports book area. Basketball, both collegiate and professional, was his favorite sport.

Hank placed bets in increments of $100, with $100 being the minimum wager. He had nowhere else to spend his money; he lost his wife several years back and had no other family, and he had money after the sale of his farm. He was also known as an avid Corn Husker supporter and his wardrobe was replete with University of Nebraska red shirts, sweatshirts, and jackets. No one saw him without his red cap. Hank stood out among the daily crowds of hundreds, if not thousands, who came through or played in the casino's sports book area each day.

A note about sports book, variously called sport book, sport books, or sports books: not all gambling casinos have a sports book; those that do usually set aside this gaming area, apart from table games and slot machines. The area is arranged in a theater setting with customers seated at narrow or small tables, while watching a large display of television sets tuned to live athletic events. Normally, except for major sporting events, two to four events could be displayed simultaneously for the customers' enjoyment, depending on his or her preference. Somewhere in the midst of all the televisions is a large display of events and wagering "odds," which reflect which team is favored to win and by what margin, as well as a listing of entries of horses in a given race and the odds on each horse to win, place, or show. In the front or to the side of the rows of seats is a counter where attendants accept wagers and pay winners.

Not only was Hank recognized as a permanent fixture in the long rows of tables where gamblers could lay out the sports section of their newspaper or *National Daily Reporter* (commonly known as the scratch sheet), he was known as a walking encyclopedia of college football and professional basketball knowledge. If you couldn't remember who the right forward was for the L.A. Lakers in 1983, Hank could tell you.

Several security officers also knew Hank. They suspected he slept in his Winnebago while parked in the parking lot that was immediately adjacent to the entrance of the sports book area of the casino. In fact, twice before the robbery and shooting they hung a courtesy citation under the windshield wiper blade reminding him of the hotel's policy of no overnight "camping" in the various parking lots that surrounded the hotel–casino complex. Other major properties in the area specifically attracted and accommodated campers and motorhomes, but not the Silver Mine. Hank sought out these officers and protested he was not sleeping there. "Okay," one said, "just don't." It annoyed Hank they'd get on his case over such a trivial issue considering the fact the casino was constantly offering him free rooms in the hotel in appreciation for his patronage.

It was known among the other "regulars" and "hangers-on" that Hank always carried a lot of money in his right front pocket, in a roll with a rubber band around it. Hank knew a wide rubber band around a roll of paper money tends to snag on the cloth pocket and it takes some effort to pull it out, a known anti-pickpocket strategy. Employees of the sports book and his friends knew how and where he carried his money. He couldn't fit the bills into his wallet, and wouldn't carry money in a back pocket anyhow for fear of a pickpocket. He knew pickpockets avoided front pockets.

A word about the sports book area and its uniqueness in this casino: Most casino operations include table games (i.e., 21 or blackjack [with variations], crap tables, a baccarat section, a poker room or designated poker area, and machines [slots and poker]) and a few casinos carve-out a sports book area. Except for the slots and other machines, which are usually scattered throughout the casino, the other attractions have their own geographical location. In the Silver Mine, the sports book area was at the very far end of the casino, furthest away from the hotel's front desk and lobby. Because of the huge size of the complex, this end of the casino had its own exterior set of glass doors leading out onto its own parking lot. Normally a guest would not park in this lot unless he or she was a sports book player. This little lot had parking spaces for approximately 250 cars. The other lots included the employee parking lot, the north lot, the west lot, the south lot, and the front valet lot. The combined lots had parking spaces for approximately 5,000 vehicles.

On February 22, Hank pulled into the sports book lot just before noon. He parked diagonally, in an end stall. He locked the doors, including the door leading into the interior of the living space of the vehicle, and walked the length of that row, past a dozen cars, toward the entrance of the casino.

February 22 was like any other day, filled with the noise of television sportscasters and roaring crowds at the televised events buttressed by the shouts and clamor of the casino patrons who, because of their financial "investment" in a given contest, are emotionally involved in each point scored or any incident that might bear on the final outcome, win or lose.

During the evening Hank went to the payout window with a big winning ticket. His cronies were jubilant over the win. A number of the patrons had long ago learned if you knew what Hank was betting on, there was a good chance you could win too. Their wagering, however, was in significantly smaller amounts. But big bets mean big wins, or big losses, and Hank often won. The exhilaration of winning is the stuff of addiction, and brings bettors back time after time. There was no secret about this day's end results. Hank was the big winner!

Among the crowd was Eddie Cunningham, always eking out a living on little jobs here and there or drawing unemployment. He too was a "regular," but wasn't included in the circle around Hank. He was, however, ever-vigilant for any tip that might help him win. February 22 was a good day for Hank, but not for Eddie. Sometime after Hank cashed in this ticket, Eddie left the sports book area.

About 10:00 p.m., there was no more interesting action and Hank was getting tired after a long day. He left the casino and headed out toward his motorhome.

Rather than getting in the driver's side of the cab he unlocked the door into the motorhome on the passenger side. As he stepped up into the vehicle and reached for the light switch he saw a dark figure lunging toward him. He instinctively raised his hands up around his face and head, just in time to partially deflect an instrument that was meant to strike him on the head. The blow struck his wrist, causing an excruciating pain, but the flow of adrenaline in a healthy and strong body ignored the blow and a violent struggle ensued. The only sound was that of grunting and gasping and an occasional curse, uttered under the breath. Two patrons on their way to their cars saw the motorhome rocking and smiled at each other without commenting.

Eddie had plenty of time, prior to Hank's arrival, to search the motorhome. He had pocketed a handful of old coins that Hank had in a jar by the bed, and found Hank's old revolver stuffed under the mattress. The gun was now tucked down into the front waistband of Eddie's pants; during the struggle, the gun fell to the floor. Eddie freed his right hand, grabbed the gun, and fired twice, hitting Hank in the head and chest. Hank went limp. Eddie jumped for the still open door, gun in hand, fell down the steps onto the surface of the parking lot, rolled over, got up, and ran across the lot in a westerly direction. Hank staggered to the doorway shouting "Stop him! Stop him!" pointing toward the fleeing assailant, with blood streaming down his face while clutching his chest. A patron in the lot took up the chase, not really knowing why, but soon gave up when Eddie disappeared.

Two other patrons on their way into the sports book area saw and heard part of the event, dialed 9-1-1 from a cell phone, and, once inside the casino, sought out the first security officer they could find. They informed her there was a serious problem and someone may have been shot in the lot. That officer used her radio and informed the security dispatcher of the report. She went to the glass doors, out onto the porch, but couldn't see anything. She used her radio to call the other officer assigned to the sports book area. The two went out and were the first security officers on the scene. There they saw a man covered with blood, stooped over on the parking lot, surrounded by several patrons.

The security dispatcher spoke with the shift supervisor, a lieutenant, who instructed her to dispatch the mobile patrol to the scene while he and one sergeant ran to the parking lot. Just as they approached the scene the first police car arrived, red and blue lights flashing. Hank, at the bottom of the motorhome steps, was now rolling over flat on his back. The police immediately summonsed the fire department's medical emergency unit.

At his time, Security Officer Shawn Carlisle arrived in the security department's patrol car. Because Hank was gasping for air, the lieutenant went to the trunk of the hotel's patrol vehicle for the oxygen equipment, but it was not there, as required. The first police officer obtained enough information about the assailant's description from Hank and one witness to send out a broadcast to other units to surround the hotel–casino complex and commence a search for the culprit. The medical emergency unit, along with three more police cars, arrived on the scene and the flashing colored lights illuminated the area. Hank was taken to a nearby hospital emergency room.

Responding police units included two police dogs that, within the hour, located Eddie buried in garbage in a trash dumpster behind the church that bordered the hotel–casino's property. A careful search of the dumpster located what appeared to be valuable old coins and a .38 caliber handgun. Eddie was wearing Hank's old brown leather jacket, something Hank had not realized during the struggle.

ASSESSMENT OF THE HISTORY OF CRIME ON PREMISES

This was a premises liability case in which the plaintiff alleges the parking lots are dangerous, especially the sports book lot, and that management was on notice it was dangerous by virtue of a long history of crimes against property and persons, but failed to provide an adequate level of security.

In the pretrial discovery process, during which both sides must surrender any and all documents and records requested by the opposing side, Silver Mine Hotel and Casino produced their daily logs (which reflect line entries of all security activity, minute by minute); all security reports of crimes for the two years prior to this event; post orders (the specific instructions for each assignment) for the mobile unit; security policies and procedures; work schedules indicating who was working at the time of the event and where; and performance records of the key security officers in the matter at hand. In addition to the records of crimes on the property memorialized by security officers, the local police department's "calls for service by location" was obtained. This is typically a computerized line item printout of every time a police unit is sent to a specific location, by date, time, reason the police were requested, and the disposition.

With respect to the history of crime on the premises, using the "calls for service by location" and security records I determined there had been 85 crimes and arrests on the property, 78 of which occurred in the parking lots, and, more specifically, nine in the sports book lot. Those crimes included assaults, thefts from and off vehicles, auto thefts, robberies, and attempted robberies. A murder had been committed in that very lot several years before, when the lot was used for employee parking. In fact, because of crimes against employees and their cars in the lot, the union insisted a security officer be permanently assigned to the employee lot 24 hours a day. Clearly, the likelihood of crime occurring was high.

The next thing I had to do was determine if the security department recognized and understood this danger and provided a reasonable level of protection.

ASSESSMENT OF THE SECURITY DEPARTMENT'S PROGRAM

Dozens of security officers worked each shift. Various security assignments and posts included the patrol of the hotel towers, the employee entrance, the dispatch desk, random patrols, lobby and front door post, gaming areas, and the exterior lots. Of all the security officers working each shift, only two were assigned outside to patrol, monitor, and protect the parking areas. One officer was in a patrol car and one in a tower overlooking the employee parking lot. However, 93% of all crimes occurred in the parking lots, yet less than 5% of the department's resources were allocated there. That didn't make sense.

The officers who were not on a fixed (stationary) post, including the outside mobile patrol, were required to report events and locations of patrol via their radios, so security management could keep track of what they were doing and where they were. Certain specific duties, such as patrolling the sports book lot and checking the pump room in the receiving dock area (tasks specifically defined in the post orders), were to be radioed in as they occurred. The post orders for the mobile patrol required the officer to drive through the sports book lot at least once an hour. The dispatcher would make a handwritten note of the call and, when radio traffic was slow, type the entry into the Daily Log, which was the official record of all events and activities occurring throughout the complex, minute by minute, hour by hour. One eight-hour shift could take several $8\frac{1}{2} \times 11$ inch sheets of paper.

My examination of the Daily Log for the swing shift of February 22 revealed there were no entries made regarding a patrol of the sports book lot. My check of the preceding day shift reflected only one entry for a patrol of the lot. In going back in time, shift by shift, for days, inspection revealed very few entries regarding this lot. That could only mean the lot in question was not being patrolled hourly, as required.

I wasn't the first person to examine the logs for evidence the lot was being properly patrolled and protected. Right after the incident, security supervisorial personnel examined the Daily Log and called Carlisle in to explain why he hadn't patrolled the lot. He claimed he did, but the dispatcher must have failed to log it. Carlisle further claimed the log entry that read "1710 (5:10 p.m.) Unit 7 (outside motor patrol) completing perimeter patrol" really meant it included the lot in question. There were two such entries on the log prior to the assault. Yet, other entries for Carlisle specifically reflected his checks in other lots, such as the employee lot and valet parking lot. Of further interest was the fact the log reflected no entries whatsoever on this swing shift for a period of over 90 minutes! Daily Logs on prior dates when Carlisle was in the patrol car also revealed long periods of time with no call-ins or reports made by him. Where was he, and what was he doing?

Not only did the sergeant and lieutenant challenge Carlisle about not patrolling that lot, he was asked to explain why the oxygen gear wasn't in the trunk of his patrol car. Post orders for the patrol vehicle specifically require the tanks be checked at the beginning of each shift to ensure they are full and ready for use in the event of an emergency. Carlisle said he forgot to check them, and if they were missing from the trunk it wasn't his fault. Indeed, Carlisle felt like he was being singled-out as a scapegoat because of the shooting. He walked out of the discussion and quit his job.

The security department also had specific orders for an hourly check of the sports book lot by one of the two security officers who were always posted in the sports book area. Both officers on that shift, Daniel Henderson and Kathryn Escalante, testified they would walk out onto the porch, every hour as required, make a visual inspection of the lot, and inform the security dispatcher each time. The porch was several steps up from the surface of the lot and, because of the elevation, the officers felt a visual survey was sufficient. But the Daily Log did not reflect the number of checks required. I stood on that very porch and the view afforded would not allow a person to really see or understand what was going on unless the activity was near the porch. I concluded a visual check fell short of an adequate security patrol. For example, that check could not and did not see the broken glass on the pavement behind Hank's motorhome. Eddie had taken an old rusty hammer and had actually broken out the rear window. He climbed in to ransack the vehicle and await its owner's return to commit a robbery (he used the same hammer on Hank in the initial assault). My contention was, had Carlisle actually patrolled that lot, he couldn't help but see the obviously busted-out rear window of a motorhome and the glass all over the pavement, and would have investigated. Such investigation surely would have discovered the criminal inside the motorhome.

THE RESULTS OF MY ASSESSMENT

It was clear to me the director of security knew that specific lot was dangerous and developed a reasonable security strategy to ensure it was frequently monitored. His requirement that the patrol car drive through at least once an hour was ignored by the patrolmen. Such employee failures are predictable. There's an old adage: employees don't do what you expect them to do; they do what you inspect. That being said, the real failure was at the supervisor level. Daily Logs are a management and supervisorial tool. Had either the sergeant or the lieutenant been reading the logs they would have found officers were not patrolling the sports book lot and could have corrected that. The truth was, no one really was paying attention to or knew what was happening in the lot and the quality of security out there was poor indeed. The truth was the check of the lot by the officers assigned to the sports book area started out as a walking tour of the lot, which would have been sufficient, but somehow it evolved into just a look-see visual check from the porch, which was easier. The security director's key staff failed him, and consequently failed the hotel–casino and, most importantly, failed a patron, Hank Fiske.

The Silver Mine Hotel and Casino filed a motion for summary judgment in the district court claiming, essentially, their security was adequate and the lawsuit lacked merit. The court agreed and dismissed the case. The plaintiff appealed to the state supreme court. The court, following its thorough review, stated, in part:

> Fiske's expert testified by way of affidavit that the security on the night of the attack was inadequate. He based his opinion upon documents produced by the Silver Mine and concluded that: (1) the prowl vehicle assigned to the Sports Book Lot had not patrolled at all during the shift in which Fiske was attacked; (2) a prowl vehicle would have discovered the broken glass outside Fiske's motorhome and could therefore prevented the assault on Fiske; (3) the visual security checks of the parking lot were ineffective substitutes for patrolling the parking lot; and (4) the Silver Mine security supervisors lacked the requisite training to properly supervise these security guards. Fiske also contends that the Silver Mine security violated its own security policies by failing to perform the required number of visual checks of the Sports Book Lot on the night in question.

The court continued saying how the hotel contended the security was adequate. It concluded by saying, in part:

> Because there are significant issues of material fact in dispute with regard to whether the Silver Mine breached its duty to provide adequate security on the evening of Fiske's attack, summary judgment on this element was in error.*

The last sentence of the conclusion of the state supreme court's decision reads:

> The summary judgment in favor of the Silver Mine is reversed, the award of costs is vacated, and this case is remanded to the district court for a trial on the merits consistent with this opinion.

The state supreme court decision regarding the foreseeability of crime remains viable case law to this day.

Following that decision my deposition was taken. I reiterated my opinions in sworn testimony. The case settled without going to trial.

---

*To preserve the integrity of the court's language it is copied verbatim, with the exception of substituting fictitious names to protect the identity of those involved.

CHAPTER 4

Marcello v. Queen of Clubs

Contents

WHAT HAPPENED?

A 21-year-old woman walked out of a nightclub for fresh air, and, while seated on the curb between two cars in the parking lot, was assaulted and beaten by unknown and unidentified young men.

WHO WAS BEING SUED, AND WHY?

The named defendants in this lawsuit included the owner of the club, the general manager, and five security officers. The complaint alleged the club and its parking lot was a dangerous place and the security provided was inadequate. The plaintiff further claimed that the security officers were not properly trained or supervised, and on the night she was assaulted, the officers performed their jobs in a negligent manner.

WHO WAS INVOLVED?

- Cindi Marcello, assault victim and the plaintiff.
- Heidi Aston, Cindi's friend who drove Cindi to and from the nightclub.
- Roberto Juarez, another friend of Cindi who accompanied both women to the club.
- Simeon Stoyanov, owner of the Queen of Clubs.
- Sahi Nawar, manager of the Queen of Clubs.

- John "JJ" Jefferson, head of security of the Queen of Clubs.
- Robert Glassman, security officer assigned to the front door.
- Phillip Robledo, security officer assigned to the front door.
- Robert Jennings, security officer in charge of the parking lot.
- Gretchen Hightower, former bartender of the Queen of Clubs.

WHEN DID IT HAPPEN?

About 1:30 a.m. on a Friday morning in August.

HOW DID IT HAPPEN?

9-1-1 operator #21 opened the switch to a call at 01:38:09 to hear a woman screaming she had been beaten and needed help. "Where are you?" asked the operator. "I'm at the Queen of Clubs in the Petersville Township," she yelled, then hung up. The call was from a payphone and the operator called that number back. The phone rang numerous times with no answer. The Sheriff Department's dispatcher was informed and a patrol unit was dispatched to the club, a location well known to patrol officers in that area.

Two Sheriff units pulled into the lot, driving past one security officer walking near the lot's entrance, wearing a bright yellow jacket with the word "Security" across the back. The units drove the length of the lot toward the front doors of the nightclub and were hailed down by a young woman, later identified as Heidi Aston. Heidi was clearly intoxicated. One deputy got out of his vehicle and asked her if she called 9-1-1. She became verbally abusive and indicated he was stupid for not knowing who really called. She said the caller was in her car. Because of what she said, how she said it, and her general condition, the officer debated whether he should arrest her for public drunkenness or not.

The second deputy stood behind his colleague, ready to assist if necessary. A small number of observers, including two yellow-jacketed security officers, gathered nearby while the flashing red lights on top of the patrol cars signaled to all a problem was at hand. The deputy couldn't make any sense out of what the intoxicated woman was saying and, in disgust, decided to leave the scene. The two patrol cars left.

While this exchange was taking place, several rows over, the caller, Cindi Marcello, sat crying in the rear seat of Heidi's car with a battered and swollen face. She told her friends two black men had beaten her, but wouldn't answer anyone's questions about more details. Her friend Roberto Juarez sat with her. Everyone had been drinking in celebration of Heidi's 21st birthday.

Heidi, along with another friend, returned to her car and drove everyone to her house. Roberto thought it was funny how she kept veering slowly to the right and had to sharply correct the car's direction because she was so "tipsy." Once there, Cindi got into her own car and drove home.

The next afternoon Cindi went to a nearby emergency room because her eye was swollen. There was nothing they could do except give her some pain pills. She then went to the Sheriff's station nearest her home and at the counter filed a report. In that process they determined she had been the 9-1-1 caller who hung up earlier that day and asked why she hadn't made her report when the officers were there. She told them she was too embarrassed.

The official version of what had transpired was now documented, as follows: Cindi stated she decided to leave the nightclub about 1:15 a.m. for some fresh air. She didn't tell her friends she was going out. When she walked out the club's front door she saw five security men together talking, all wearing their yellow jackets. She passed them and proceeded at an angle to a row of cars at the edge of the parking lot, nearest the street, where Heidi's car was parked. The cars in that row bordered and faced the street. The edge of the lot was designated by a curb, behind which laid a grass strip, then a sidewalk, another grass stripgrass, and the street. She sat on this curb between two cars with the grass strip to her back with her feet on the surface of the parking lot. While sitting there she heard what sounded like a zipper being opened and turned around to see, within a foot of her, two young men, one with his hand on the zipper of his pants. They laughed. She told the deputy who was taking her report that she used derogatory language in telling them to get away from her. They left and she continued to sit there looking toward the nightclub. According to her, the two men returned within a few minutes and immediately commenced to strike her with their fists about her face and chest until one told his companion "Okay, she's had enough," and the two again left the scene.

Once they left her, she stood up and could see the small group of security men, still standing in a circle about 150 feet away. She didn't call out or inform them as to what occurred. Rather, she walked toward the center of the mall and found a bank of payphones and dialed 9-1-1. During that call she decided she didn't want to discuss the matter and hung up, and only now, hours later, wanted to make a formal report.

Shortly thereafter she sought out an attorney who filed a complaint against the nightclub for failing to provide a sufficient level of security to protect its patrons from criminal assaults. I was retained by the law firm representing the nightclub and asked to review all available material to determine whether the club was negligent or not.

ASSESSMENT OF THE PLAINTIFF'S CASE

When the defense attorney told me the plaintiff's version of what happened I was immediately suspicious. Why didn't she report the two men to the security officers who were close by? Or, if she didn't think their conduct was worth reporting, why not move to a location closer to the security officers? Why didn't she scream or call for help when being pummeled? Why didn't she scream for help when the two men left her and point them out as assailants? Why didn't she run to the security officers and report what had just happened? Why did she call 9-1-1 then hang up? Why didn't she go to the Sheriff's vehicles when they came into the lot and report what had happened? She knew they were there, yet she stayed in Heidi's car.

My task as a security expert is to impartially and objectively assess the facts and arrive at an opinion as to what happened and identify failures, breaches, omissions, or negligence, if they exist, irrespective of which side retains me. If, in my view, this young woman was victimized because of security negligence, I'd tell the defense lawyer. Many times, when retained as a defense expert, I've been obliged to say, "You don't want me on the witness stand as your witness. If the right questions are asked, I'll answer them and sink the ship." We would then part ways and the lawyer would go off looking for another expert. Regrettably, "experts" are out there who will say what the attorney wants to hear. Some have that very reputation, as "hired guns."

In the vast majority of lawsuits that I've been engaged with the plaintiff was truly a victim of a crime. The focus isn't on whether the plaintiff is telling the truth or not, but, rather, was security (or the absence of) the proximate cause of the crime. Indeed, even when defense attorneys and experts suspect some deception, care must be taken so as to not alienate the jury. Example: If a woman claims she was forcibly raped, and there's a belief she had consensual sex, challenging her could backfire if the jury accepts her story and is sympathetic with her. The lesson here is to accept the story and concentrate on the security-related issues.

In this case, my suspicion was heightened when I read Cindi's deposition testimony. In that forum, now two years after the incident, her version of what transpired was remarkably different from what she reported to the Sheriff's Department. She testified that while sitting on the curb she felt a wetness on her back and turned around to see two young black men, one with his penis in hand, urinating on her. What she said and did thereafter was in keeping with her original version. I would consider being urinated upon as an outrageous affront, which would evoke an emotional outburst that could be heard a city block away. But, no, she testified she did not scream or call out for help, but used profanity in telling them to get away and used the "N word" and remained seated on the curb (all wet in urine) until they returned and beat her.

There's no question Cindi had been beaten, but I was privately convinced it didn't happen the way she described it. It was pure speculation on my part, but I suspected she had left the club with a man. They got into a car in the lot. While inside the car the man made a proposition that she rejected and as a consequence he ended up striking her several times. I did not, nor could I, share that suspicion with anyone. Heidi, Roberto, and the other friends who all rode in the crowded compact car with Cindi testified in their depositions that they did not smell any urine as they drove home. Not overpowering evidence one way or the other, considering the condition of the celebrants!

ASSESSMENT OF THE SECURITY PROGRAM

Not long after being retained I told the attorney I'd like to meet him at the club, see the area where the assault allegedly occurred (including its relationship and distance to the front door where the security officers were standing), and meet the owner, manager, and security officers. The club didn't open until 8:00 p.m., so we agreed to meet at 7:00 p.m.

The attorney and I met for the first time. We stood in the lot and visited for five minutes or so and then headed for the entrance to the club. The first person I met was the club's manager, Sahi Nawar. My heart sank. I had come to learn that many jurors tend to like or dislike—therefore, believe or disbelieve—a witness based on the witness's appearance. Sahi simply looked sinister. Coal black hair slicked-down, long narrow sideburns, and a goatee. The only thing missing was a scar across his cheek. He was a pleasant and intelligent man, but not warm and fuzzy. We talked about his strategy of always having two men in the lot and two men at the door. The one doorman checked identifications of incoming patrons to ensure they were of age, and the second doorman stamped each patron's hand with an ultraviolet image after the guest had paid the cover charge. He told me the lot was divided in half, for patrolling purposes, and each man made a continuous oblong loop around his section of the lot.

During this conversation, at the entrance, the owner drove up in his Mercedes. My heart sank a second time. I wondered if the young attorney had the same emotional reactions I was experiencing. Simeon Stoyanov was a surprisingly young-looking 35-year-old who appeared to have stepped out of the pages of *GQ Magazine*. Simeon was an impeccably dapper, almost regal, and handsome man wearing an impressive diamond ring. Would the jury look kindly upon this king of a roaring nightclub with the liquor flowing and scantily clad girls in crows' nests gyrating to loud music under the colored lights above the crowd? I was skeptical.

Simeon was also pleasant and articulate. He expressed implicit faith in Sahi—Sahi was in charge and if Sahi said two men were necessary for the protection of patrons in the lot, then he'd pay for two men. One, in his view (and mine) would have been sufficient, but Sahi wanted two.

Later I came to learn the city council had decided to rescind the nightclub's license because of frequent fighting in the lot, requiring the Sheriff's Department to spend time and resources unnecessarily. Upon appeal, spearheaded by the club's corporate attorney (not the attorney selected by the insurance carrier for the defense in this lawsuit), the council issued a new provisional permit on the condition two security officers would always be in the lot. The club was in compliance with the provisional permit.

About this time a few patrons started arriving, although the club was not yet open. One woman, about 30, pulled her station wagon into a stall and patiently sat in the vehicle smoking a cigarette with all the windows up. What was most remarkable about her was the station wagon clearly appeared to be her home. Personal effects, including a tea kettle, were jammed into the interior, blocking all windows except the two front doors and windshield. There must have been a cave burrowed lengthwise for sleeping purposes in the midst of all the belongings. Here she was, ready for an evening out in a nightclub!

While security officers Robert Glassman and Phillip Robledo started to set up their tables at the entrance I was introduced to John "JJ" Jefferson, the head security officer. He was an imposing figure, 6′5″ tall, who only spoke when he answered questions and even then with as few words as possible. I did learn from him, if a patron inside became disruptive or there was a problem, that patron would be escorted to the door. Each officer carried a radio. One of the outside parking lot guards would be informed if someone was being ejected to come to the door and complete the escort to the person's car.

The last security person I met that night was Robert Jennings, who was the "senior" security officer in the lot on the night the incident occurred. He said the assault, as described by the plaintiff, did not or could not have happened. He was in that portion of the lot closest to the club's entrance, which included the site of the assault. He was adamant and angry over the lawsuit. A former U.S. Marine, Jennings had been a door host in another nightclub prior to joining the Queen of Clubs. He was a physical fitness buff who exercised with weights on a daily basis, and had a family and a dog. What a consultant won't learn while talking with witnesses!

I was shown the exact location in the lot where the plaintiff claims she was beaten. I measured the distance at 150 feet from where Glassman and Robledo were stationed. That's 50 yards, a sand-wedge shot. The incident occurred at 1:30 a.m. when there's little traffic on the street next to the lot. One could hear the sound of normal conversations at that distance at night, although they couldn't distinguish the words. Any scream or shout would have caused attention.

In my review of all the documentation and testimony, I determined a policy had been established at the club whereby every noteworthy incident in the lot would be written up in a report, but the policy wasn't followed.

Among the evidence I reviewed was the testimony of Gretchen Hightower, a former bartender at the club. She stated the security officers drank on the job. She knew because she served them, and Sahi knew they drank. In fact, free drinks were part of the benefit package. A second former bartender said the same thing. They also stated that officers assigned to the lot would come in, leaving the lot unattended, to have a free drink. Sahi and Simeon denied this, claiming both Gretchen and the other ex-bartender had been discharged and it was their way of getting even with the club. Each security officer denied this, stating they were professionals, it was their livelihood, and they knew drinking would interfere with their performance as well as safety in dealing with agitated, aggressive, and intoxicated patrons.

MY DEPOSITION

There was nothing remarkable about my deposition. The plaintiff's original attorney had brought in another trial lawyer to assist her. Some attorneys have the skills and talent to try a case, but many don't. Bringing in that kind of talent meant the attorney's fee for any award given by the jury would be shared between the attorneys. Usually a plaintiff lawyer gets one-third of an award for their fee for services rendered. The remaining two-thirds goes to the plaintiff, less the expenses, which can be sizeable. For example, the plaintiff had to pay my hourly fee for the time of the deposition. Expert's fees can run into hundreds of dollars for each session. Some cases may have several experts on each side.

I testified to the following:

- Some of policies and procedures of the security organization were not being followed; however, not writing reports had nothing to do with this incident.
- The lot had a long and continuous history of fights and violence, but two officers in that small lot far exceeded any parking lot security coverage I had ever seen, and fights between patrons do not represent the same danger as predatory-stranger crimes.
- The security training provided by the club was minimal, at best, but each employee came to them from other clubs and bars so they were all experienced.
- If security officers (or door hosts or bouncers) drank, it would fall below the standard of care in the hospitality industry and be totally unacceptable.
- Security officers should never commit perjury because perjury was a crime.
- Nightclubs should never hire persons who are convicted felons.

Finally, I testified that I did not believe the plaintiff's version of what happened, and I was of the opinion the security strategy in place at the time of the incident was adequate.

THE TRIAL

The trial lasted three weeks. The plaintiff's case is presented first. When the plaintiff rests (concludes) then the defense calls its witnesses. It should be noted expert witnesses are rarely, if ever, present during a trial. Their only appearance is when called to the witness stand to testify and that's planned—for example, "Mr. Sennewald, we expect to call you to the stand on Thursday, probably after lunch."

As the trial progressed I had occasion to talk to the attorney I was working with and he indicated he was not happy with the progress. He sensed the jury didn't like Sahi or Simeon. Then he told me the shocking news that the plaintiff had impeached (discredit one's truthfulness) Jennings (the security officer in the lot) on the witness stand. During Jennings deposition he was asked if he had ever been convicted of a crime. Jennings testified he had not. Through their investigative efforts, the plaintiff discovered his conviction for selling drugs (the drug was a steroid used for body building). They knew the answer before the question was asked and Jennings fell into a trap by lying while under oath.

While on the stand I reiterated my earlier deposition testimony and, again, agreed there were operational failures by the club's staff and there was a need to conduct background investigations of applicants for security positions and felons should not be hired into security positions. Again, I testified I did not believe the plaintiff's version of what happened. "Well, Mr. Sennewald, if you do not believe my client as to what she testified under oath happened, do you know with certainty, what in fact did happen?"

My only answer could be and was, "No."

"That's because you weren't there, is that correct, Sir?"

"Yes," I answered. "But Ms. Marcello was there, wasn't she?"

"And she has told us what happened, hasn't she?"

"Yes," I replied.

"Thank you Mr. Sennewald, I have nothing further."

This skilled cross-examiner left the suggestion in the jury's mind that his client's version of what happened was really unassailable; it must be correct! The defense counsel could have risen on a redirect examination to rehabilitate that concluding exchange but chose not to. There are times you simply must stop and trust the jury to grasp some of the subtle differences between fact and fiction, which are invariably present in a trial.

The jury found for the plaintiff and awarded her $18,000. Considering the time and expenses connected with this lengthy litigation, it was but a fraction of what the plaintiff sought. The defense attorney considered that a win. I suspect the two attorneys representing the plaintiff were shocked by the small size of the award, and may have not considered it a professional victory but a financial disaster. I considered it a loss, although it was apparent to me the jury found not *for* her, but *against* the club.

CHAPTER 5

Chatálet, et al. v. FantasyForest, Inc.

Contents

WHAT HAPPENED?

While at a bachelor's party, a small group of FantasyForest male employees were shown a videotape of FantasyForest female entertainers in various stages of undress while in their dressing room. Another employee had secretly videotaped the women as they changed for various acts. The mystery employee also filmed the restroom in the women's dressing area. The matter was reported to the security department, who allowed the situation to continue for another two months while they identified the culprit and developed a strategy to catch him in the act.

WHO WAS BEING SUED, AND WHY?

FantasyForest, Inc. (a major theme park) and various senior executives, including Robert Laughlin, vice president of security and safety, were named as defendants in a lawsuit alleging they carelessly and negligently responded to the complaint that someone was surreptitiously watching and recording female employees in the privacy of their dressing room and restroom. The plaintiffs further alleged the investigation was unprofessional, ineptly managed, and conducted with no sense of urgency or prioritization, which allowed extended and continued victimization of the young women.

WHO WAS INVOLVED?

- Marie Chatálet and eight other FantasyForest entertainers.
- Ted Simpson, FantasyForest's lighting technician and one-time fiancée of Marie Chatálet
- Robert Laughlin, the director of security and safety for FantasyForest.
- James O'Hare, the security manager for FantasyForest.
- Gus Lombardi, FantasyForest's stage manager.
- Clifford Beckman, a security investigator.
- Wayne Stevenson, the wardrobe and costume technician who was caught in the act of videotaping female entertainers in the Fort's dressing room.
- Barney Poole, the wardrobe and costume technician who owned the video camera.
- Paul Cork, the Boone County deputy sheriff assigned to FantasyForest as a liaison officer.

WHEN DID IT HAPPEN?

The first taping was in the late spring. The bachelor party viewing was in late September. The matter was first reported to a stage production manager on October 1. One week later, it was reported to security and safety. Wayne Stevenson was caught in early December.

HOW DID IT HAPPEN?

The balcony of the apartment was the only smoke-free area and it too was packed with the groom's fellow employees. It was a BYOB (bring-your-own-bottle) party and invitation was by word of mouth. It was assumed everyone was an employee of FantasyForest, but you couldn't really tell because the word spread among various departments and not everyone was known. Wayne Stevenson and his friend, Barney Poole, showed up around 10:00 p.m. Wayne had a videotape in his coat pocket. Neither of them knew anyone's name, but they recognized faces in the crowd. After locating the VCR and ensuring it worked, Wayne and Barney moved about the apartment and tried to shout above the crowd that a "dirty movie" was going to be shown in the dining room in five minutes. The announcement didn't generate anywhere near the interest Wayne had imagined.

About a dozen men stood by, either holding a drink or with arms folded, when the videotape started. It was obviously an amateur production, candidly taken of a group of young women in various stages of undress, changing costumes. Ted Simpson emerged from the bathroom in time to see his fiancée, Marie Chatálet, walk across the screen. He immediately identified the group as the female entertainers at work, obviously in their dressing area. He was shocked. He was grateful Marie was not undressed. In looking at the small crowd, no one seemed overly concerned nor did anyone seem to recognize Marie. How can anyone get a camera in there? he thought to himself. He was privately outraged, but others were having a good time. "Hey, look at those boobs, Harry. Isn't she the one who slapped you last month," evoking laughter among the group. There wasn't anything really explicitly obscene in the tape, but Ted thought it was probably illegal and certainly in bad taste.

When the tape was over and the crowd dispersed Ted approached Wayne and told him he could get in serious trouble showing a video-tape like this. He also asked Wayne how he obtained the videotape. Wayne laughed and said he had his "ways." Ted didn't know Wayne's name or department, but he did recognize him as an employee. He broke off the discussion by again warning Wayne he could be heading for trouble if he didn't stop taking such videos. Barney stood by during this conversation.

Ted fretted over the videotape the rest of the weekend. On Monday he shared what happened with coworkers who weren't at the party, asking what they would do. The consensus was it should be reported to the stage manager, Gus Lombardi, who was on vacation but due back in one week. To report it to someone else would violate the chain of command.

When Gus returned to work the next week, Ted told him about the event. Gus asked him who the man was who had the videotape and Ted said he didn't know his name, nor did he know the name of the short, heavyset man who followed him around. He said he thought the two might be in the wardrobe area, but wasn't sure. Ted said the only thing he did not want was to be identified as an informer against another employee.

Gus said he'd talk to his boss about how to handle this and would get back to him. Several days later Gus told his boss, and he was instructed to take the matter to the security and safety department. Gus had an appoint-ment set up with the security manger that afternoon.

James O'Hare had Gus take a seat after they shook hands. Gus informed the security manager of his conversation with his subordinate. Gus asked if he knew the identity of the offender and videographer. He didn't. "Where does this man work?"

"We don't know," said Gus.

"What's he look like?"

"Gee, I have no idea. I wasn't told."

Of course the security manager asked for the name of the employee who had seen the videotape, but Gus told him he wanted to remain anonymous. "Look, Gus, I can't proceed unless I have more information. You go tell your guy to come see me."

Later that afternoon, Ted sat with O'Hare and told him what he saw and what was said between himself and the employee who had the camera that night at the party.

"Who else saw the videotape?" asked O'Hare.

"I really don't know, maybe a dozen guys, all employees here I think," replied Ted.

Ted described the culprit. Before the day was over, the story offered by Ted was typed into the form of a sworn affidavit. "We require this affidavit before we can proceed," Ted was informed. He signed it.

The investigation was now official and underway. It was October 7.

ASSESSMENT OF THE SECURITY DEPARTMENT AND ITS INVESTIGATION

The discovery process produced, among other documents, the "FantasyForest Security and Safety Policy and Procedure Manual." The section on "Investigations" ranked among the most professional and comprehensive of all such manuals I've seen in the private sector. I was suspicious it was in part plagiarized from a public sector agency, not because of quality but because of content. For example, they claimed their crime laboratory could do microscopic comparisons of all kinds of evidence from striation markings to handwritten and typewriter imprints annalists, and could do moulage and plaster of Paris castings (make 3D imprints of footprints), as well as having latent fingerprint expertise. These activities are simply not found in security departments. Later this presentation of professionalism made sense when it was disclosed the director of security and safety was Robert Laughlin, a recently retired special agent in charge of the local FBI office. The security department, of course, did not have such technical expertise.

Laughlin had no real involvement in or understanding of the security industry, and it appeared he was brought aboard as window dressing and good public relations for FantasyForest. On what grounds could I possibly arrive at that conclusion? Of great significance was that Laughlin had no knowledge of any investigation into this invasion of privacy. How could the director not know of such an important investigation? He was never informed of nor was consulted with about this matter. He didn't ask his security manager what was happening of interest or what was significant or a problem in the organization. Instead, he attended civic luncheons as a speaker and was involved in other community programs that generated goodwill for FantasyForest. He identified and associated with senior management and rarely was seen in the security offices. He delegated all operational activities to O'Hare. Anyone in management knows one can delegate authority and assignments, but one cannot delegate responsibility.

O'Hare was a retired policeman from a midsize city on the east coast. He had no managerial experience and very limited investigative experience. He started as a uniformed security officer at FantasyForest. He assigned the invasion of privacy case to Clifford Beckman, one of his "investigators."

Beckman was a retired highway patrolman from the midwest. He, like most members of the department, came to the area for the climate and subsequently sought some interesting employment to supplement his retirement pay. He, too, started as a uniform patrolman at FantasyForest and was subsequently promoted to "investigator." His only investigative experience was in auto accidents. That limited focus of investigations isn't all bad; the investigative process is universal: it's the search for who, what, how, where, when, and why. So, by following the process, he should be able to solve this case.

Beckman started at the most logical place, the Fort's dressing room for the female entertainers. The room was on the second floor of a huge structure. The third floor was the elevator and electrical and mechanical equipment room. Was there some opening that would allow a person to view down into the dressing room from that area? No, he determined. The building was tiered, so one could walk around the third floor on the roof of the second floor and walk around the second floor on the roof of the first floor. In the wall of the second floor, Beckman found a 3-foot by 3-foot metal access door into the HVAC (heating and air conditioning) machinery area. The door had a faulty lock and he could enter. Inspection of the darkened interior required a flashlight, even though one could turn on a bare 40-watt light bulb hanging by the ducts. He could find no way to view the interior of the dressing room.

Immediately adjacent to the dressing room, with a common wall, was a communication center for all the radios used by employees throughout the large theme park. Because of the vital importance and sensitivity of this equipment room, it was protected with an intrusion alarm—that is, the door was protected with alarm contacts and every time that door was opened an alarm sounded at the security department dispatcher's desk. Upon receipt of the alarm, a security officer would be sent to investigate.

Despite this protection, Beckman inspected the common wall and discovered numerous small holes had been intentionally drilled to see into the dressing room. There was evidence of footprints on various pieces of furniture and the long workbench against the wall indicating where some person or persons stood and with one eye could view the interior of the dressing room. He also found a location where a viewer could get to the top of this wall and look over and down into the restroom. Clearly these women were being watched with some regularity.

But Beckman was perplexed. He could find no opening or hole large enough to accommodate the lens of a video camera. There had to be another location from which one could watch and videotape.

A reinspection of the interior of the dressing room disclosed a standard, secured access panel from the room itself into a hollow space of sufficient size to allow a worker to access more of the HVAC air ducts. Once inside, there was another hanging bare 40-watt light bulb with a switch.

Maintenance workers would have known of this, but the wall between the space and the dressing room was solid except for an electrical outlet that was mounted on the dressing room wall. The electrical wire to the outlet looked loose. Beckman, flashlight tucked under his arm, examined the wire and, to his surprise, the plate came loose. He could move the electrical plate (the same type everyone has in their home to either plug in an appliance or switch a light on or off) from its backside and view the interior of the room. From that vantage point he could also see the open door into the restroom. The plate was actually the cover plate of an air conditioning control knob. Beckman had found the location where the peeper/employee could videotape the women. Disturbances in the dust all around this switch area and the floor beneath it substantiated the discovery. This was a "Bingo!" He immediately radioed O'Hare informing him of his discovery. O'Hare wasted no time to drive to the Fort and joined Beckman in the dressing room.

They determined that the cover plate had to be completely removed from its normal position in the wall to allow for the lens of a camera. That meant the culprit would get into his position behind the wall between performances or before the first act of the day. While in there, he would push the plate into the room and it would dangle there held by the two electrical wires connected to the switch. If you were inside the dressing room and looked at that wall and noticed the switch, it would appear as though it had fallen from its normal position on the wall and needed to be pushed back in, or one might think it was being repaired. Who would imagine there was a man and a camera behind the wall peering through that hole?

It was then and there O'Hare made the decision to allow the condition to remain so as to catch the peeper in the act. In his view, the position of the switch plate was the key. All that had to be done was routinely check the switch plate. If it was hanging down it meant the culprit was in his position and had no way out except through the access door right in the dressing room. The peeper would be trapped! An order was issued to have the uniform patrolmen assigned to the Fort make hourly checks on the wall switch and report it to the main security office if it was hanging down.

So now security knew that someone was peeking into the room from two sides and from above. The where and how were known. The why was apparent. The challenge now was who and when. This was day two of the investigation.

The next step was to identify the voyeur.

Several days later, Ted, while walking toward the employee cafeteria in the underground maze of tunnels, ran into Wayne and stopped him. "Still shooting the women?" he asked.

"All the time," responded Wayne, with a big smile. Simpson really had hoped to get Wayne's full name off his employee badge. All he could read was "Wayne."

"They're gonna get you, one of these days."

Wayne said, still smiling, "That'll be the day!" and off he went southbound down the main tunnel.

Ted called O'Hare and told him of his encounter with Wayne. Based on this information Beckman went to human resources for a search of the computerized listing of 1,422 employees looking for the first name of Wayne. There were three. One, Wayne Stevenson, was in wardrobes and costumes, which was located in the southern part of this underground city that served as the "behind the scenes" of the theme park, housing all the offices, maintenance machine shops, generators, supplies, storage, and employee services. Only security was headquartered aboveground.

Stevenson was 22-years-old, lived with his parents, had been with FantasyForest for two years, and was rated as an average performer. His file also reflected a complaint made against him for rubbing a female employee's breast while he was fitting her for a new costume. She was positive he did it intentionally, but when confronted with her complaint he insisted it was accidental. Wayne was warned he must be careful during fittings; any new similar complaints could lead to serious disciplinary action.

Beckman decided to have a criminal background check made through the sheriff's department and spoke with the liaison deputy assigned to the park, Paul Cork. Cork checked law enforcement records and later that day advised Beckman that Wayne had been cited and fined for possession of an open alcoholic beverage container in an auto when he was 18-years-old and, two years later, was arrested for trespassing at night near a women's dormitory. He pled guilty to this minor offense, was fined $100, and given eight hours of community service. When Wayne completed his application for employment at FantasyForest he answered "yes" to the question about criminal convictions and wrote "trespassing" on the form. That did not raise a red flag then, but now, in light of the current situation, that conduct and conviction was meaningful. "Trespassing at night" could indicate he was a peeping tom, a true voyeur.

Beckman and O'Hare discussed the status of the investigation. Beckman said he wanted to call Wayne in and confront him. O'Hare said no. "What if the kid denies it? You have no evidence. If he sits there and stares you down and doesn't admit it, you have egg on your face and have to put him back to work. Then he'll never do it again and the matter goes unsolved and the tapes he's been making are still in circulation."

Beckman responded, "If he sits there and denies it, then I'll bring in Ted Simpson who witnessed the showing of the tape."

"Yeah, but if the kid's smart and still denies it, it's one employee's word against another, and you can't take any action under those circumstances. We have no other person who was present at that party willing to come forward and verify Ted's information. No, we must catch him in the act, and then we'd have grounds to search his home and recover all tapes, which are likely in his possession. Be patient; the next time he slips into that space we'll have him."

Weeks passed and no security officer called headquarters to report the plate hanging loose. Neither O'Hare nor Beckman went out to talk with the various patrolmen to ensure they knew the importance of the check. Nor was anything done to seal the holes in the wall between the communication room and dressing room. Employees accessing that communication room were authorized to enter and could bypass the alarm, so the strategy in place to catch peepers ignored or overlooked that risk. The same was true with respect to the restroom ceiling that was still vulnerable to someone looking down. Everything was in a state of suspense pending the call from a patrolling officer, which never came.

The entertainers were oblivious to the entire matter, and simply assumed the dressing room provided to them was secure and assured them the privacy to which they were entitled.

In the meantime, Ted had another chance encounter with Wayne and, this time, Wayne indicated he had just obtained some spectacular shots of the women. Ted wasn't sure if it was true or Wayne was just trying to get under his skin. O'Hare was again contacted, and this newest information was shared. Beckman was called in; he had been actively engaged in a mysterious disappearance of blank bank checks from the controller's office, and the invasion of privacy case was on the backburner.

Ted's report of his encounter and discussion with Wayne forced the investigators to again focus on the Fort. The discussion resulted in the decision to request funds for a camera that would pick up images in very low-light conditions, an infrared lamp that would help illuminate the interior space (a light that could not be seen by the suspect), and a new recorder with a monitor. The plan was to install this equipment and conduct an electronic 24-hour-a-day surveillance.

If Wayne entered he would be captured on videotape, even if the investigators weren't there. Wayne could deny his activity all he wanted, but the evidence of the tape would prove otherwise. The request for the equipment was formally processed up the chain of command.

The first approval signature had to be Robert Laughlin's. He signed it without asking the purpose of the equipment. With Laughlin's approval, the purchase order went its rounds until all required signatures were obtained. The corporate purchasing agent called and, after a discussion with O'Hare, ordered it. Two weeks later the shipment arrived.

The next evening, after the entertainers had gone home, Beckman, assisted by another security investigator, entered the space and within four hours mounted the camera, installed the infrared light, and ran the camera's coaxial cable over the dressing rooms ceiling and into the communications room. There they connected to the VCR and tested for the picture on the monitor. Beckman had his colleague crawl through the access door from inside the dressing room and make his way to the wall plate. Beckman, watching the monitor, could see his colleague, but couldn't make out details; details weren't necessary. The installation was successful, and the around-the-clock monitoring began at near midnight, Wednesday night. It was now the first week of December.

The next morning Beckman brought O'Hare to the Fort to show-off his installation. They entered the communications room (i.e., the same room in which holes in the wall were being used and one could climb up and peer into the restroom) and approached the monitor. Beckman was immediately startled to observe what he thought was his partner in between the walls and wondered why he was in that space. He used his radio and called his partner who answered promptly. "Is that you?" asked Beckman, clearly puzzled by what he was seeing and hearing. "I mean in the wall?"

"In the wall?" asked the younger investigator. Then it was shockingly apparent the dark silhouette of the man in the space was the culprit! "I can't believe it," whispered Beckman as they both stared at the monitor, "we've got him already!"

O'Hare nodded in agreement. On the other side of the wall they could hear the women chattering. All the women had arrived at work. Wayne had entered earlier to await their arrival.

Both O'Hare and Beckman wondered what he was doing. As the two investigators watched the monitor it became clear Wayne was masturbating as he watched through the switch plate opening. Then they could see him raise a camera to the opening. For the next 40 minutes Wayne would put the camera to the opening, then pull the camera away, as though filming only the best scenes then waiting for more good shots.

When the women left for their first performance, Beckman and O'Hare hurried out of the communications room and entered the dressing room. They opened the access door and called for Wayne to come out, telling him he was under arrest. Wayne crawled out and was taken into custody then transported to the security offices. The camera was, of course, immediately seized and the cassette was removed for evidence.

Once inside the security building, the trio went to O'Hare's office where the interrogation was to be conducted. There were many questions that needed answering, including when the filming first began, how many times Wayne had been in that space filming since the bachelor's party, what he did with the videotapes, how many videotapes he made, etc. But, before the questioning could get under way, Deputy Cork, who had only a fleeting understanding of what the security investigators were working on, overheard the voyeur was in custody in O'Hare's office. Cork went to the office and opened the door. Beckman announced they had caught the employee in the wall space recording the entertainers. Cork asked if the camera had a microphone and if voices were recorded on the videotape. They all examined the camera on the desk and it indeed picked up sound. "In that case," announced Cork, "this case falls within the sheriff's department's jurisdiction. Recording others without their knowledge is a federal violation, and I must take custody of the prisoner and the evidence."

The security officers were stunned. Security made arrests regularly. Such offenses as thefts from vehicles in the parking lot, shoplifting from the various gift shops, pickpockets, use of stolen credit cards, or passing counterfeit currency were almost daily occurrences that ended in so-called "citizen arrests." The sheriff's liaison officer assisted, and only upon request. Cork's intervention in this matter came as a shock.

Wayne was whisked away, along with the camera and videotape. Now Laughlin was notified of the events, but it was too late. Later, the sheriff reported Wayne confessed to the taping and that only one tape was recovered from his bedroom, claiming it was the only one he ever had. Wayne pled guilty to an illegal interception of communications charge, a misdemeanor, and received a light sentence that included psychological counseling and community service.

Following the arrest by security, the sheriff's department interviewed each dancer and they were allowed to view the videotape that was recorded just before the arrest. The dancers were outraged with what they saw and learned, especially the news that Wayne had been suspected weeks before his capture and they were allowed to be victimized and exposed to this man for such an extended period of time. They also came to learn of the holes in the other wall and the vulnerability of the restroom. They sought legal advice. When Marie learned that her fiancée had seen her on a videotape in September and didn't tell her or warn her, she broke off their relationship.

Once the lawsuit was filed the park modified its "FantasyForest Security and Safety Policy and Procedures Manual" to include a regularly scheduled survey and inspection of all restrooms and dressing areas on premises, to ensure there would be no repeated or similar problems. The walls and ceiling of the entertainer's dressing room in the Fort were repaired.

MY ASSESSMENT OF THE SECURITY DEPARTMENT'S STRATEGY

My review of all the various documents, including the history of prior criminal events on the premises, disclosed numerous peeping tom incidents, including the catching of a maintenance man drilling holes through the wall between the communications room and dressing room just one year prior to this case. That employee was terminated, but no one bothered to cover or fill the holes. Other cases, including the detection of an employee who constructed a position in the ceiling over a public women's restroom installed his own ventilation grill to watch through, clearly signaled that voyeurism was an ongoing threat to this kind of facility, and there was a need for a program of restroom inspections for breaches of privacy. But no effort had been undertaken, after either case, to prevent this activity.

In my deposition testimony I was critical of the strategy that relied on a uniform patrolman to monitor the wall plate. I pointed out that if they didn't have the cameras, which could pick up images in the dark (contrary to the policy and procedures manual that indicated they had the whole range of investigatory equipment), that didn't preclude them from using the alarm technology that was right at hand. The communications room door was wired into the alarm system. All they had to do was install common sensors on the inside of the access door by rerouting two wires and whenever that door was opened an alarm would signal to the alarm board in the security building. It was that simple.

"Well, Mr. Sennewald, what experience do you have in solving voyeur problems in the workplace?" asked the defense attorney.

"I've had my share when I was a security executive, and I successfully resolved them in a timely manner," I replied.

"Can you cite for me an example?"

"Surely," I replied, and I referred to my book titled *The Process of Investigation: Concepts and Strategies for the Security Professional*, in which I described a case where a store detective smelled fresh wood in a stockroom behind fitting rooms used by female customers in the swimwear department. The detective followed her nose, finding fresh sawdust on an upper shelf. Standing on the lower shelf she could see someone had recently drilled a hole into a fitting room. She contacted me. In a matter of hours I determined the best suspect was a new maintenance man who had been noticed staring at female employees. I devised a scenario for the next day in which the suspect would be summoned to the personnel manager's office to replace a light bulb. While he would be on the ladder making that change, the manager of the swimwear department would enter the office and inform the personnel manager her swimsuit had just arrived, and ask her if she could come right down and try it on. The personnel manager said she would. As planned, the maintenance man overheard all this and almost broke his leg getting down and folding up his ladder. A few moments later he was caught with his eye to the hole. The case was resolved in a span of two days.

I did not fault the security investigators for "losing control of their case and their employee suspect." They were foiled by an overzealous sheriff's deputy. However, because of that improper intervention, no one will ever know if more videotapes are out there and in circulation. There is no peace of mind for the victims in this case.

I found no fault in O'Hare's rejection of Beckman's proposal to interview Wayne early on; that was good judgment.

I was critical of Laughlin for not having a hand in the management of his own department, for not being abreast of important problems in the facility, and for not being cognizant of how an important investigation was being handled, all of which contributed to the extraordinary delay in the case. I noted the delays subjected the women to weeks of unnecessary invasion of privacy. In my opinion, the lack of leadership, the absence of a sense of urgency, and the early investigative strategy fell below the security industry's standard of care, and the investigation was unnecessarily delayed and negligently conducted.

The matter settled out of court.

McCortney v. Sky-High Casino

Contents

WHAT HAPPENED?

A man walked into the Sky-High Casino, approached a total stranger play-ing a nickel slot machine, pulled out a .38 caliber revolver from a holster covered by his sweatshirt, and shot the player in the head, instantly killing him. The shooter then turned and walked out of the same doors through which he had just entered moments before.

WHO WAS BEING SUED, AND WHY?

The decedent's surviving family members, who were present and play-ing slots next to the victim, filed a lawsuit against the Sky-High Casino, a small local casino and restaurant, on the grounds the casino was a danger-ous place based on prior criminal incidents, that the security staffing was inadequate, and the security officers were negligent in allowing an armed man to enter the casino without being challenged.

WHO WAS INVOLVED?

- Carl McCortney, the victim, a 50-year-old man who had just retired and was in the process of buying property in Duncan for the purpose of relocating there with his family.
- Dean McCortney, a resident of Duncan, who was playing the slot machine next to his brother at the time of the shooting.
- Jim Hutchinson, the security officer assigned to the casino floor.

- Larry Wright, the security officer assigned to the parking lot.
- Robert Cassidy, the security sergeant who was eating in the restaurant at the time of the shooting.
- Robert Bennington, a Duncan police officer who was eating with Cassidy.
- Harold Hauffman, the shooter.
- Charlie and Betty Miller, patrons of the casino, accompanied by their friends, Mr. and Mrs. Ochoa.

WHERE DID IT HAPPEN?

Sky-High Casino, a single-story wood-frame building, is located in a small community 20 miles from the nearest metropolitan area. The primary clientele are locals. Meals served in the casino's restaurant are old-fashioned home-cooking and are inexpensive. It's where the local police eat or stop for coffee. The building faces a main east–west thoroughfare, but the front door is seldom used. The south, or back side, of the building faces onto a parking lot and most people enter through that back door. Upon entry through the first set of double glass doors, there's a small game room to the right for those under age who are not allowed into the gambling area. Immediately thereafter is the second set of double glass doors opening directly into the casino.

The parking lot has a maximum capacity of 500 vehicles. South, across the street from the parking lot, is a rundown motor court of the 1930's and 1940's era. At the time of the shooting, each bungalow was rented to people of low income, most of whom were on some form of government assistance.

WHEN DID IT HAPPEN?

Based on the security videotape's date and time generator and the patrons' reactions to the exploding sound of the gun shot, the shooting occurred at 1:37:30 p.m. on a Tuesday afternoon in June. The exact time will be an important factor in this litigation.

HOW DID IT HAPPEN?

Harold Hauffman, age 39, lived in cabin #6 in the motor court just south of the casino complex. His cabin is the third and next-to-last unit on the left of the two rows of eight cabins that comprise the rental property. He was unemployed and lived on his monthly disability check.

Harold was dressed in a filthy gray sweat suit and wearing rubber thongs. Strapped on his waist was a leather belt and holster with a .38 caliber revolver in the holster. Just prior to the shooting, Harold proceeded up and north between the two rows of cabins, crossed the street to the casino's parking lot entrance, walked north toward the back door of the kitchen section of the casino, then west along the back side of the building toward the back-door entrance. Along that route he passed a black-and-white Duncan Police Department patrol car parked in the "no parking" zone by the kitchen's door. His route brought him to the sidewalk that continues out of the casino and along the handicap parking zone. Harold walked along the front of those cars parked in the handicap stalls, each car facing the wall of the building, then turned right on the sidewalk to the first set of glass doors. He pulled the right door open and entered the foyer. Just as he entered, the Millers and Ochoas entered the foyer as they were leaving the casino on their way to the parking lot. As Harold passed this group he bumped into Betty Miller, somewhat jolting this senior citizen to the point she gasped in disbelief as to the rudeness as well as the apparent filthy condition of Harold, who appeared to be in a rush to get into the casino.

"Goodness! Did you see that man? Did you see how dirty he is? Disgusting!" commented Betty as they entered the parking lot, now headed in an easterly direction along the same route Harold had followed in the opposite direction.

"He looks just like Charles Manson," observed Mrs. Ochoa.

Harold entered the casino, stood there for a "moment," then turned to his left facing the end of a long row of slot machines banked along the south wall of the building. All the machines were being played. Seated at the end machine, closest to Harold, was Carl McCortney. To Carl's right was his brother, Dean; to the right of Dean were Carl's wife, Millie, and other members of the family, a party of six in total.

Harold suddenly pulled out his revolver and, at point-blank range, fired the weapon at Carl's temple, instantly killing him. Not a word had been spoken. The bullet traveled through Carl's head and fell harmlessly on Dean's shoulder. Carl immediately slid forward off the stool and fell in a heap on the floor in front of the machine. At the sound of the explosion, Dean looked in the direction of the sound, to his left, to see and feel Carl slipping off the stool, and at the same time saw Harold reholstering the gun as he turned and walked through the first set of glass exit doors. It took a few seconds for Dean to process what had happened and realize the shooter was leaving the scene. He ran to and through both sets of doors in time to see the shooter walking on the sidewalk, not 30 feet away, toward the lot. As he ran through that small foyer and out the exterior doors he was shouting, "Stop! Stop!"

About five minutes prior to the shooting, Security Officer Jim Hutchinson reentered the casino from the cafe holding a Styrofoam cup of coffee. He had left the floor for a couple of minutes to get the coffee. Hutchinson was standing in the "pit area" and had stopped to watch a blackjack game. From that location if he looked to his right he could see the back doors, which were 80 feet away. In fact, he could see out into the lot through the doors. When the shot rang out he looked in the direction of the doors and saw people ducking. He first thought it might have been a car backfiring. He started walking in that direction and then saw a man run to the doors shouting "Stop!" That man exited running, apparently after someone. Hutchinson started running, too, through the casino toward the doors, after the man who shouted "Stop!"

Sergeant Robert Cassidy and Police Officer Robert Bennington were seated at the lunch counter when they heard the shot. They looked at each other, but both assumed it was a car backfiring. Someone at the restaurant door leading into the casino shouted "Someone's been shot," and both men bolted toward the back kitchen door to get out into the lot and approach the casino from the south side. Cassidy knew the way through the kitchen and was followed by Bennington.

The Millers and Ochoas were still walking together slowly. They left the sidewalk and were walking behind the handicap parked cars talking about this rude man and how he even had Manson's wild hair and beard. As they walked, their conversation was interrupted by shouting coming from behind them. They turned to see Harold running toward them as he pulled out his gun. The group watched in stunned silence as another man tackled him to the pavement and the gun went flying and skidded along the surface of the lot. A uniformed guard, who looked like he was chasing the man running behind Harold, jumped on the two entangled on the ground. Now three were struggling and scrambling for the gun. As the two couples stood there in utter disbelief, two more uniformed men came up from their rear, from the kitchen area. One picked up the gun and the other helped the other two restrain the wild-looking man wearing a gray sweat suit. The two elderly ladies both had their hands covering their mouths.

Then, running toward them from the eastern portion of the lot, came yet another guard. Suddenly, a police car with red and blue lights careened to a stop near the police car that had been parked by the kitchen. Within the next several minutes two more police cars arrived, as did a fire rescue unit.

Charlie Miller told every policeman who walked or ran by that he and his companions had witnessed everything. Their statements were eventually taken.

Harold was handcuffed, escorted back into the casino, and taken into the employees' lounge. After he was advised of his "rights" he was asked why he shot the man. He said he didn't shoot a man, he shot the "source."

"Source of what?" asked the detective.

"The source of the vibrations that were driving me mad," replied Harold.

Harold explained he had been having a problem with vibrations and earlier he was watching television and the vibrations returned, hurting his head. He followed the vibrations out of his cabin, across the street and into the casino, where he found the source. Harold shot the source. He looked and sounded mentally ill.

The area around the body of Carl McCortney was cordoned off with yellow crime scene tape. Other than this 200-square-foot crime scene zone, the balance of the casino returned to business as usual. A few stood by and watched the police photographer taking her shots, crime scene technicians taking measurements and sketching the scene, officers interviewing witnesses, and the eventual removal of the body, but most patrons returned to their slot and video poker machines.

At the police station the investigators had the unpleasant task of questioning Harold. He had a strong, unpleasant body odor and terrible bad breath. His toe nails were long and dirty, as were his fingernails. Harold kept talking about the maddening vibrations and how he followed them right to the casino and to the source. He said he had to bring to an end this evil source. Detectives obtained a search warrant and went to cabin #6 later that afternoon. The door was still ajar and the television set was still on, but the channel only reflected a test pattern. The interior of this cabin was, not surprisingly, filthy. Even veteran police officers were shocked to find 14 plastic gallon jugs filled with urine. Harold wouldn't explain why he was saving it. Clearly, he was mentally ill.

Harold was transferred to and incarcerated in an institution for the mentally ill where he remains to this day. The state considers him incapable of standing trail for the murder of Carl McCortney.

The family felt justice was denied by the criminal justice system, so they looked to the civil process for satisfaction. A multimillion-dollar lawsuit was filed against the casino.

ASSESSMENT OF THE PLAINTIFF'S THEORY OF LIABILITY

The plaintiff had the burden to prove the following:
1. The casino was a dangerous place based on the history of crime on the premises.
2. Because they knew it was dangerous they had a duty to provide a reasonably effective security program.
3. Two security officers and a sergeant actually working was not a reasonable level of protection, in fact it was inadequate.
4. Considering 1, 2, and 3, the violent death of Carl was a foreseeable event.
5. The negligence was the proximate cause of the shooting. Put another way, but for the inadequate security, the shooting would not have occurred.

The plaintiff retained a security expert, who testified in deposition that one important contributing factor of proof that the security was inadequate was the numerous calls for police service at that casino. Clearly, the mere volume of requests for police indicated an extraordinary crime problem at that location.

A careful examination of each call revealed four general categories of calls:
1. Many calls reflected on the computerized printout had to do with police officers going out of service to eat; calls to "meet the officer" (one policeman wanted to meet and talk with another policeman with no indication or suggestion a crime had occurred); police officers requesting a tow truck; and officers making highway stops where the traffic offender either voluntarily pulled onto the casino's parking lot or stopped in front of the building on the highway (to identify where a motorist is stopped the nearest street address is used in the computer).
2. Of those calls that were clearly for crimes requiring police attention, most were for theft of autos or theft from autos in the lot or fender-benders in the lot. Time and again, it's been established the most "dangerous" part of any facility, business, or institution is the parking areas.

3. There was only one stranger-predator crime in the past three years, a parking lot purse snatch. Stranger-predator crimes against persons are an important indicator of the level of danger in any environment. One such crime in three years, even in view of numerous crimes against property, typically wouldn't rise to the level of classifying a property as "dangerous." There were also fights and assaults, but always among family, friends, or acquaintances.

4. In three years there were several calls about the presence of guns, knives, or other weapons, or where someone threatened to injure someone else. In each case, the calls to the police from the security department were advisory (e.g., "A tall, thin man wearing a black bowler hat just left our casino and a friend tells us he's carrying a .45 caliber handgun in his boot") or requesting assistance (e.g., "We have a drunk in custody, threatening people he's going to go home and get a gun and come back and shoot everyone. Maybe you want to take him down and lock him up?").

The expert for the plaintiff claimed these incidents indicated the casino was dangerous. I disagreed. In my view it was no more or less dangerous than any other similar property.

The plaintiff's expert testified two security officers were not enough to provide an adequate level of security. He felt five would have been a sufficient number. The focus on the fact that only two were "working" was buttressing the impression that only two were on the premises. The third officer in the restaurant was as much a part of the protection force on duty as was the police officer having lunch at the counter a part of the police deployment for the city that day. And not only did the casino have three security officers on duty, there was a police officer on the premises!

One must be reasonable in terms of the number of security officers on duty at any given time; for example, five security officers were indeed assigned to the evening shift on weekends and holidays because of the anticipated number of patrons. A Tuesday afternoon has substantially less traffic and less need for security manpower. Two officers, one inside and one outside, on a weekday in this small casino was adequate in my view. I walked the casino floor at a casual pace and could cover the entire area in five minutes. I then walked the parking lot in the same fashion and could cover the entire lot, easily, in less than 15 minutes. The third officer served as a relief and extra coverage, including typical gaming area security needs, such as "fills" for machines and escorts.

The plaintiff's expert testified (in deposition) that this crime was fore-seeable, not only because of the history of crime, but because the casino was located in a neighborhood in which crime generally was "highly foreseeable."

Interestingly, prior to this case, the plaintiff's expert had defined crime foreseeability into four levels or categories: (1) a crime was not foresee-able, (2) the crime potential was low, (3) the likelihood of a crime was moderate, or (4) the likelihood of a crime was high. In his definition of high-crime areas, he described how one could tell if a neighborhood was of high-crime foreseeability by a pattern of assaultive crimes and that the buildings and structures had to exhibit evidence of security precautions like bars on the windows, alarm boxes, perimeter fences, abandoned autos with broken windows, graffiti, and a general bad reputation.

The neighborhood in which this casino was located had none of these characteristics. The motor court behind the casino was in need of paint and renovation, but it was the only property in the area that needed attention.

When my disposition was taken I mentioned this contradiction between what he wrote and what he testified to in this case. "I just wish your expert would practice what he preaches," was my testimony.

So, in this matter, I testified the security strategy for this property was adequate, the property was not a dangerous place, the neighborhood and area was not a high-crime area, and this bizarre event was not foreseeable. Lastly, the time it took for this tragic event to unfold was measured in sec-onds. There could have been ten security officers on duty and it still could have occurred.

There was a dispute over whether the holster and gun was visible as Harold walked across the lot and into the casino. Those who saw him prior to the shooting made no mention of seeing a gun. Had the Millers and Ochoas seen a gun they surely would have mentioned it. The wearing of a large leather belt and holster on top of the solid gray sweat suit would be conspicuous. Absent anyone seeing that, I was of the belief he had the sweat shirt pulled down over this gear and only revealed his intentions at the last second.

But even if Harold had walked into the casino with the gun and hol-ster in plain view, which some people did from time to time, a security officer would approach that person and advise him or her that the car-rying of a weapon was against casino policy, and that it would have to be checked or removed from the premises. This was written policy and prac-tice. Nor would such an event cause any alarm. Although Harold would be recognized as a "low-life" character dressed as he was, with wild and wooly hair and beard, it doesn't suggest he's dangerous and about to kill someone, let alone a stranger. Indeed, the investigation of Harold's background disclosed he had entered a major upscale hotel casino in the state conspicuously wearing his holster and gun and he was stopped and questioned by security. They checked with the police in that city and verified that Harold had a valid and current permit to carry the weapon (but not concealed). In that instance, he was asked to leave the property or have the weapon checked and he chose to leave. That occurred a year prior to this shooting.

There were 10 cameras mounted around the casino. The cameras were part of a sequencing system, all recorded. Sequence timing was on a one-minute cycle, meaning each camera scene lasted five seconds until the next appeared, taking one second between each scene. It took 60 seconds to complete the full cycle. Camera #1 viewed the door through which Harold entered. Camera #2 focused on the south wall, including the location of the shooting. So if the camera monitor displayed the door at 1:36:00, it would view the door until 1:36:05, then switch to camera #2 from 1:36:06 to 1:36:11, and so on for the various camera locations. The best evidence as to the actual time of the shooting was on camera #8 when a dealer ducked below her table at 1:36:46.

Careful examination of the videotape disclosed that Harold was not in view of cameras #1 and #2 between 1:36:00 and 1:36:11, nor was he in view of those two cameras when the cycle came full around to 1:37:00 (at the door) and 1:37:11 (at the crime scene). That meant he could only have been inside the casino between 1:36:11 and 1:37:00, or a maximum of 49 seconds. Remember, the plaintiff was critical of the fact security did not approach the murderer and either eject or disarm him once he entered the casino.

This incredibly short timeframe was further confirmed by the elderly foursome who had encountered Harold when he bumped into them on his way in. They walked, uninterrupted toward their car in the parking lot until their attention was attracted to the pursuit behind them. They had covered approximately 50 yards from the back door. Twice I retraced their steps, slowly, and timed how long it would take me to get to where they said they turned and witnessed the tackling of the shooter. Each test was just over 80 seconds. Of course my speed could not be confirmed and was speculative at best, but, nonetheless, it confirmed how quickly the entire event unfolded, and the unreasonableness of the plaintiff's criticism of no reaction and intervention by casino security.

Following the discovery and taking of the expert's depositions, several settlement conferences were held. Resolution of civil lawsuits comes through a trial by the court (judge only, no jury), trial by jury, binding arbitration (the matter is presented to an "arbitrator," a jurist or attorney agreed to by both sides) who renders his or her irrevocable decision, or by settlement. Settlement is simply the process whereby the plaintiff and defendant agree to an amount of money that will satisfy both entities, which brings the lawsuit to its conclusion. Oftentimes the amount of settlement is confidential and may not be revealed.

This lawsuit reached a settlement.

CHAPTER 7

Crane v. Major Stores, Inc.

Contents

WHAT HAPPENED?

A customer, accompanied by her two young children, opened a bag of candy, store merchandise, to pacify her children during a lengthy delay while a sales associate attempted to locate an item in the stock area. When the purchase of the big-ticket item was concluded, the sales associate assisted the customer by pushing the item out of the store in a shopping cart. Once outside, the customer was detained for the theft of the candy by a loss prevention (security) agent, escorted back into the store, and, in the office, was obliged to sign an admission of theft before she could leave.

WHO WAS BEING SUED, AND WHY?

Major Stores, Inc., its officers, store management, and loss prevention agents were sued for false arrest, false imprisonment, and extortion.

WHO WAS INVOLVED?

- Joelle Crane, the customer who was detained.
- Danny Crane, Joelle's four-year-old son.
- Tina Crane, Joelle's two-year-old daughter.
- Bob Burkhart, the sales associate who sold Joelle the television set and assisted her out to the parking lot.

- Greta Voorhees, the relief cashier who witnessed the removal of the candy from its display and observed the customer opening the bag and giving candy to her children.
- Harry Glikman, the loss prevention agent who detained Joelle and required her to sign an admission of guilt.

WHERE DID IT HAPPEN?

Major Stores, Inc. is a chain of discount stores with a front-end checkout configuration, similar to check stands in a supermarket. Three departments—electronics, jewelry, and the pharmacy—have their own cash registers. This store was located in a suburban neighborhood of a major metropolitan area.

HOW DID IT HAPPEN?

Joelle Crane picked up both children at their daycare center and decided to make a quick stop at the store to purchase her husband a portable television set for Father's Day. She had seen the ad and the price was compelling. The sales associate, Bob Burkhart, said to her, "You're fortunate, madam, this is the last set we have. It was on display, so I'll have to get the original carton and accessories … it'll only be a couple minutes."

"Thank you," she said, as she looked over at the two toddlers who now sat happily on the floor. "Oh, no, no, babies … the floor's dirty. Don't sit there. Mommy will be done in just a couple minutes and we'll go home."

Tina started to cry, "I want to go now."

"Me, too, mommy. I don't like it here and I'm hungry," said her brother.

The mother gave a wan smile, "In a minute, the man will bring us daddy's present and we'll go home. Don't you want me to get daddy a present?"

"Uh- huh," they both chimed in.

"But I'm hungry," repeated Danny, "and I want to go home."

"Me, too," echoed Tina, who intentionally plopped back down on the floor and started to cry softly.

Bob came back to the counter and said, "I'm so sorry, I can't find the power pack to the set. Please bear with me, and I'll find it."

"Please!" pleaded Joelle, now concerned that the children were becoming overtired and the delay was starting to wear on them. Danny started whimpering and the two couldn't be quieted or consoled.

Joelle saw a display of packaged candy hanging on a rack across the aisle and thought such a treat might pacify the children until she could conclude her transaction. I'll just take the candy and pay for it when I pay for the television, she thought. She removed the package of candy, priced at 79 cents, and the children calmed down with the treat.

Bob reappeared, asked for more time, sounding quite frustrated with his inability to locate the battery, and again disappeared. After more delays Bob finally presented the complete boxed set and, even though almost all sales are made at the checkout stands, major purchases such as this are transacted in this big-ticket department to accommodate the customer.

Bob recorded the sale, but didn't know about or include the 79-cent candy package. By that time, Joelle had forgotten about the candy and was pleasantly surprised to hear she didn't have to stand in line at the cashier stations at the front of the store. Upon completing the sale the Bob said, "Thank you so much for your patience, Mrs. Crane. Please allow me to carry your purchase to your car."

He placed the carton in the shopping cart, along with both children. They bypassed the checkout stands and passed by the store's door greeter. Not far from the door, much to Bob's surprise and certainly to the agitation of Joelle, Harry Glickman stopped them and, after identifying himself as an agent of the loss prevention department, asked Joelle, "Didn't you forget to pay for something?"

"I don't think so," she answered, puzzled by the question.

"Does the word 'candy' ring a bell?"

She looked dazed, then spoke, "Oh my, yes. I'm sorry. I completely forgot about the candy. I'm so sorry."

"Well, we'll give you a chance to fix that, if you'll simply follow me please," and they all returned to the store, pushing the basket. They passed the checkout area where Joelle could pay for the candy and continued, much to her distress, because the children were starting to become restless again. They reached the rear of the store and entered into the security office.

"Why do I have to pay here," she asked, "instead of at the registers in front?"

Ignoring her question, Harry asked for her identification. "Why do you want my identification for me to pay for the candy?" she asked, mystified by the events. Harry held out his hand, expecting the identification. Joelle opened her purse and placed her driver's license in his hand, mostly out of wanting to expedite this matter as quickly as possible.

"Mrs. Crane," commenced Harry, "all I require from you is your signature on this form, admitting the theft, and we'll let you go on your way."

"Theft?" she gasped. "What theft?"

"Theft of the candy," replied Harry calmly. "We call it theft when you eat our merchandise and don't pay for it. What do you call it?"

"I call it a mistake, that's what I call it, and I take great exception, sir, to you suggesting I stole anything. I'm not signing any form that states I stole anything. I want to pay for the candy and leave immediately. My children are tired, I'm tired, and I'm leaving. Where do I pay?"

Harry was not moved, "Mrs. Crane, you don't understand. You either admit you failed to pay for the merchandise or I'll have no choice but to call the police."

"This is outrageous! Let me use your phone to call my husband."

"You may not call anyone. Either you sign this admission or I must call the police. And let me point out, Mrs. Crane, if you force me to call the police, they'll have to take your children to the juvenile unit for their protection and safekeeping."

Mrs. Crane broke into tears, and, upon seeing how upset their mother was, the children also started crying.

"My God, what's this all about over some candy?" She turned to Bob, who was stunned by the events unfolding before him, but was speechless.

"This can't be. I can't sign something that isn't true. I didn't try to steal anything. Please, let me call my husband."

Harry refused the request again, and, in the clamor, crying, and near-hysteria, Joelle signed the form so she could leave with her children.

Prior to the confrontation outside the store, Greta Voorhees, a relief cashier, had noticed the well-groomed woman with her two little children in the appliance section on her way to the employees' lounge. She even thought to herself how hard it is to shop with such little children. She should have those tikes in daycare, if you ask me, she thought to herself. After visiting with coworkers and polishing off a soda, she returned to the front, and there was the same customer. Now the kids were crying. Yeah, see, she confirmed to herself. Then, to her surprise, she saw the woman walk over to a candy display fixture, remove a bag of candy, open it, and give each child some of the candy. Bet she forgets to pay for that candy, she thought, and then, of all people, there was the loss prevention agent, Harry, coming around the corner.

"Harry," she said, "quick, let me show you a lady who has our candy in her hand that she just took off the rack."

Sure enough, Harry could see what Greta was reporting. "How do I know she didn't pay for it?" he asked.

Greta responded, "Man, I watched her. She walked right to the fixture and took it. How could she pay back there?"

That question sounded reasonable to Harry.

"Watch her," Greta said. "I'll bet you she doesn't pay for it."

Harry took up the challenge, deciding to maintain constant surveillance to see if the customer was going to pay for the candy or not. A short time later the customer dropped the now-empty cellophane candy bag into a trash container, and Harry recovered it as evidence.

Only big-ticket items could be recorded at the terminal in the electronics department, so Harry knew the lady had to go to a front checkout stand to pay for the candy. She didn't; instead, she and the sales associate bypassed that area as they left the store. This wasn't a risky or complicated matter. The customer admitted outside she hadn't paid for the candy; that's simple theft. All he had to do to satisfy company policy was to obtain her written admission, which released the store from any liability, and she could leave. To his amazement, the customer wouldn't admit to the language on the preprinted form that read: "… removed the merchandise from the store without paying for it."

He shook his head, "Good grief, the merchandise was in her children's stomachs. What was so wrong with the language in the preprinted form? Clearly our merchandise is in the kids' stomachs and it left the store without being paid for."

All he wanted to do was get the release so he could release them. He ignored, forgot, or was never trained in the use of discretion and reasonable good judgment that can be exercised in extraordinary circumstances.

ASSESSMENT OF SECURITY POLICIES AND PROCEDURES

The store's basic policy for detaining a customer for shoplifting stipulated the agent was to personally witness the theft and that all customers were to be referred to the police. If there was any compelling reason for not calling the police, such as one's health or age, the accused shoplifter could be released if he or she signed a pre-printed admission form.

Harry didn't understand this policy, nor was he properly and adequately trained. He violated Major Stores' detention policy in a number of ways, starting by taking the word of another employee rather than witnessing the "theft" himself. Properly-trained retail loss prevention agents are taught not to detain on someone else's word; professional agents must actually witness the theft before taking action. Indeed, most "bad stops" are based on the word of a third party. There's an old adage in retail loss prevention and security, "If you didn't see it, it didn't happen."

Store policy regarding the disposition of shoplifters was in keeping with industry-wide practice—that is, referring detainees to the police or, under certain circumstances, releasing shoplifters after obtaining an "admission and release" form. It's only logical that if you detain a person for shoplifting and he or she admits it, the store has no liability. In this case, Harry had an admission of guilt, but a refusal to accept the language on the admission form. Policy didn't address these circumstances, and the company failed to give Harry guidance on dealing with this foreseeable set of circumstances.

MY ASSESSMENT

My assessment, summed-up in both my deposition testimony and testimony from the witness stand during trial, was as follows:

Store personnel had every right to stop this customer and ask her to return to the store to pay for the candy. If the store felt some form of release was necessary, then a simple handwritten statement stating she inadvertently forgotten to pay would have been sufficient. She could have paid and that would have concluded the incident. If she still refused to even sign a brief statement, the receipt generated by a cash register (if allowed to pay) would be a form of documentation and that, coupled with a statement from the sales associate who witnessed all this, would have sufficed.

This loss prevention agent didn't handle the matter in an appropriate or acceptable fashion. His threat to have the customer jailed and have her children taken from her if she refused to sign an admission of theft was clearly a form of extortion. Security personnel cannot, and never should, make any promises or threats in obtaining admissions or any other form of cooperation from a person accused of theft.

THE VERDICT

I was later informed the jury was outraged over the agent's threat to have Mrs. Crane's children taken from their mother over the candy, which she didn't take with criminal intent. They saw that as wholly unreasonable and mean-spirited. They considered the agent's behavior extortion and punished the store with a whopping award heard throughout the retail industry.

This was yet another case in my long career where a store's security or loss prevention agent's egregious treatment of a customer accused of shoplifting outweighed the serious issue of theft from a store.

This very case was one of several which prompted me to write the book *Shoplifters vs. Retailers… The Rights of Both.*★

★ Charles Sennewald, *Shoplifters vs. Retailers: The Rights of Both.* New Century Press, 2000.

CHAPTER 8

White v. Mid-American Inns

Contents

WHAT HAPPENED?

An airline crew checked into a hotel following their last flight for the day. Within a short time, one of the attendants was sexually assaulted in her room while her colleagues waited for her in the lobby.

WHO WAS BEING SUED, AND WHY?

The hotel was named in the lawsuit for inadequate security and security negligence.

WHO WAS INVOLVED?

- Mary White, a relatively new flight attendant.
- Ron Hefstedder, copilot and member of the flight crew of five who checked into the hotel.
- Bobby Sonderman, retired chief of police and expert witness for the plaintiff.
- An unknown male assailant.

WHEN DID IT HAPPEN?

Within an hour after the flight crew checked into their respective rooms, sometime around 8:00 p.m.

HOW DID IT HAPPEN?

The plane's passengers had disembarked, and the crew of five had completed their day. A van took them to the contracted hotel, and they went through the quick check-in procedure. The desk clerk handed the three flight attendants their keys and the captain and second officer their keys. All took the elevator to the fifth floor and went their various ways with the agreement they'd assemble in the lobby in 45 minutes after freshening up to share dinner together. Mary White entered her assigned room and, upon discovering the room didn't have a coffeemaker, she left her luggage and returned to the desk, explaining her desire to have a coffeemaker. Rather than have someone deliver the appliance, she was reassigned to a new room on the fourth floor, just one level below her colleagues. With two keys in hand (her original key and the new key), she went to her new room to check it out. A coffeemaker was present. She left that room, rode the elevator up one floor, returned to her original room, gathered up her uniform, coat, and suitcase, and returned down to her new room.

Her intention was to return the key to the fifth floor room once she met her coworkers in the lobby. On her way to the elevator to descend to her new room, she saw the copilot in the hall and informed him of her change of rooms and the new room number.

She unlocked the door to her room on the fourth floor, which opened and swung to the left, hitting and stopping against the west wall of the room. The light switch was immediately to her right on the wall facing the length of the room. Further to her immediate right was a doorway (without a door) leading into the toilet, tub, and shower. In front of her and slightly off to the right was the sink, counter, and stack of towels. From the back of the sink counter to the ceiling was lattice work that you could see through; on the other side of this ornamentation was the coffeemaker. The space between the wall on the left and the end of the sink was the entry to the main part of the hotel room which included the bed, which was off to the right.

Mary headed for the sliding-glass door at the far end of the room, passing the bed to her right. She was still pulling her wheeled luggage. Her intention was to open the slider, which opened onto a small balcony overlooking a central courtyard. She wanted fresh air in the room. As she approached the slider she heard something behind her and, upon turning, was startled to see a man dressed completely in black, including a ski mask, long sleeves, and gloves.

Mary dropped the handle of the luggage as he seized her arm and jerked her toward the sofa, which was against the wall and adjacent to the bed. She was instructed to disrobe and sit on the sofa. She later told the police she was utterly terrorized. While seated, he took of his pants, threatened her, and forced her to perform oral copulation.

As this was occurring, the rest of the crew had gathered in the lobby and were waiting. Because she was late, Ron Hefstedder, the copilot, went to her room. As he approached her door he noticed it was slightly ajar and the key was still in the lock. He gently pushed the door, but it would only open an inch or two because the privacy chain had been engaged. Ron called Mary's name through the crack of the slightly opened door. She later told the police the assailant forcibly prevented her from answering.

After calling her name, the copilot informed Mary her key was sticking out of the lock. He heard a male voice answer, "Oh, Okay. Sorry, I'll get it."

Puzzled by the sound of a man's voice, Hefstedder nonetheless left and headed for the elevator to return to the lobby. Some few steps away from the door he heard her door close behind him. He turned and noted the key was no longer protruding from the lock and the door was shut.

He told the waiting crew what he had seen and heard, and decided he must have gotten the wrong room number and went to the desk. The desk clerk was on the phone. Ron could hear a woman screaming over the phone. He recognized the voice. The clerk picked up a second phone and dialed 9-1-1; the police happened to be in the neighborhood. The first police officer entered the lobby a few minutes later. The copilot raced back up to the fourth floor and observed a hotel maintenance man knocking and shouting for Mary to open the door. She refused and could be heard yelling for him to get away from the door. Later Mary said she thought he was culprit.

When the police arrived on the fourth floor, they too asked her to open the door. She said she couldn't because all she had was a towel wrapped around her. Eventually she opened the door and, after the paramedics arrived, she told all concerned what had transpired. She had the presence of mind to preserve the evidence, which she spit into a vial provided by the paramedics.

Mary's room was taken out of service for as long as was necessary, knowing the matter would surely cause the filing of a lawsuit.

Mary filed a lawsuit against "John Doe" (the assailant) and the hotel for inadequate security for travelers in general and female guests in particular. The complaint was subsequently amended to include another "cause of action"—negligence—after the plaintiff's counsel discovered the hotel's master key had been missing for four days prior to this incident. Clearly, the plaintiff's position was someone employed by (or formally employed by) the hotel had intimate knowledge of the hotel, its operations, security, and the fact that airline attendants regularly stayed there.

The plaintiff further contended the assailant waited with the master key for the most attractive target of opportunity, and the plaintiff was his choice. The plaintiff would take the strong position that a missing master key was a matter that should have created a greater and urgent concern among the hotel's management because it posed a serious risk to every guest, not just to women. No one would stay in a hotel knowing the master key was missing. The plaintiff retained Bobby Sonderman, the former chief of police of the southern city in which this hotel was located, as her security expert, and counsel for the hotel retained me as the hotel's security expert.

ASSESSMENT OF THE HOTEL'S SECURITY PROGRAM

This was a pretty straightforward case, on the face of it. Clearly, the missing master key would be hard to explain to a jury. I credited the hotel for having a key control system that "caught" the fact the master key was missing, but faulted the hotel for allowing four days to pass without rekeying the locks. Rekeying a hotel is a major expense, therefore a reasonable period of time is needed to fully investigate and attempt to locate the key, but four days could not be justified. Here was another example of finding some contributory negligence in a defense case and I shared that "bump in the road" (i.e., bad news) with the attorney defending the hotel. That sharing meant if I was asked while under oath if it was negligent to allow four days to pass with a master key missing, I would be morally and legally obliged to say "yes." That would not bode well for the hotel.

It really wasn't an issue of inadequate security in terms of the number of security officers who were or should have been on duty, or the quality of security officer training. Indeed, there was a well-trained security officer on duty at the time of this incident, engaged in his regular routine of patrolling the floors.

The focus of the case wasn't the issue of foreseeability of crimes based on a history of criminal incidents. I checked all available hotel records and police data, including calls for police service at that address (a good indication of the frequency of police and crime-related incidents), and there was no indication it was a dangerous location. I know Sonderman checked the same data (or should have). Historically, and from all other perspectives, this was a clean, above-average, airline-approved place of lodging in a fairly crime-free part of the city. It would be foreseeable that a guest could be victimized if an unaccounted-for master key was in the hands of some employee or friend of an employee.

The police pursued their objective of attempting to identify the assailant, while Sonderman and I pursued our objective of determining if the hotel was civilly liable for the attack. In the police's pursuit they checked every possible suspect, including all male employees of the hotel, for DNA comparisons to the semen evidence. There were no matches. The detectives were mystified by the suspect's M.O. (method of operation). No similar crime had ever happened in this major city.

Further, the police investigation failed to locate the key to the room. Indeed, there should have been two keys, the one for that room and the key to the fifth floor room that White had yet to return to the front desk. There were no keys. If, indeed, the master key was used it's likely the culprit wouldn't want to carry it away and possibly be stopped with it in his possession. It would be better to leave the key or all keys in the room.

Each expert, if he or she wants to or knows what he or she is doing, conducts what is called a *site inspection*—that is, a careful visual inspection of the property and crime scene to better understand the entirety of the event. That's weighed against the police report of their findings and their record of what the witnesses and victim tells them. Comparing all this information against the victim's sworn deposition can reveal interesting or curious differences that can give direction to the search for the truth of what happened.

The plaintiff told the police how she had changed rooms, and, after inspecting and liking the second room, she left the light on because she knew she'd be right back after retrieving her luggage from her original room on the fifth floor. She had to turn on the lights to see and ensure it was satisfactory, and to ensure it had a coffeemaker.

In her sworn testimony, she said she returned to the second room and, upon entering, turned on the light switch so she could see, as anyone would do upon entering a dark room. Subsequently, during her sworn testimony, she stated when she returned to the fourth-floor room with her luggage and entered the room she had to turn on the light.

MY ASSESSMENT OF THE EVENT

My focus concentrated on her and her story of what happened. I became privately convinced her story wasn't entirely truthful. These are the issues that struck me as peculiar:

1. No one, including the police, questioned the desk clerk if Mary requested a room change, especially on a different floor from her colleagues, or if the change was the desk clerk's doing.

2. An assailant attired in 100% cover up, allowing absolutely no descriptions, is suspicious, particularly in cases of sexual assault. She couldn't even give the idea as to the race of the culprit.

3. Why did the plaintiff offer two different and contrasting versions about whether or not the room light was on? If she left the light on, wouldn't she be suspicious to see the room dark when she returned within minutes?

4. How could she keep semen in her mouth for so long? How could she hold it in her mouth during the phone call to the desk shouting for help, shouting through the door, and talking to the police and paramedics?

5. What happened to the keys?

6. Why didn't she scream initially or as soon as the culprit left the room and run out into the hallway screaming?

7. Could this be a setup to convince everyone she was a crime victim—that is, a male confederate, already waiting in the hotel, checked into another room waiting for her signal to act? And couldn't she have left the key in the lock in her haste and anxiety over the drama to be played out, and the co-conspirator was already in the room waiting? Aren't there a number of possible combinations of this kind of scenario?

8. Could a co-conspirator provide the semen that she could mouth from a vile or other container and spit it out at the right time?

9. Wouldn't it be unusual for someone in this horrific type of crime to have the presence of mind to hold semen ejaculated into one's mouth by an assailant and stranger? Wouldn't one spit it out as soon as possible? Couldn't that spit be gathered and preserved as evidence in the forensic survey of the crime scene?

10. No one, in the brief time from the copilot hearing a man inside the room, to his decision to check with the desk clerk when he heard Mary screaming for help on the phone, to the various parties arriving promptly, saw any person dressed in black leaving. Could that be because the "assailant" was a registered guest?

In trial, Sonderman, as I understand it (normally experts are not present in the courtroom when opposing experts testify, principally because of the costs involved), testified the master key was used, unequivocally, and the hotel was negligent. His bottom line was, but for the failure to remedy the missing key, the plaintiff would never have been assaulted. During his cross-examination he was asked if he had any hand in the training of the police detectives during his service. He did, and he praised their investigative skills, including the quality of the investigation into this sexual assault. His final point was that he believed the assailant saw her enter the room the first time and, believing she was returning, let himself in with the master key and waited for her return. Then he donned his black costume once inside.

Therefore, the plaintiff's expert formed an opinion as to how the event unfolded and connected the event to the negligence of the hotel's control of and reaction to a missing master key. He shared his opinion with the jury.

When I was questioned about the missing master key, I agreed it was wrong of the hotel not to change all the locks, irrespective of the expense, but I doubted the master key had any role in this alleged incident. In my opinion, master keys have a greater value for surreptitious use for financial benefit or even for a more natural sexual attack than this one-time unusual attack. I could not share with the jury my suspicion of a setup, which I couldn't prove, for fear of alienating and/or angering someone on the jury. After all, it was pure speculation. I did testify I couldn't explain some of the very unusual and peculiar circumstances of this event, hoping the jury would also be curious about such evidence as the semen in the mouth.

I was never asked, on the stand, if I suspected the incident had been staged.

Toward the end of my testimony, and I was the last witness, the questioning went something like this: "Mr. Sennewald, you're aware, are you not, that Chief Sonderman, the plaintiff's expert, testified before this jury that his opinion is the assailant had the master key, chose Ms. White as his victim, let himself into her room, and waited for to return? You understand that sir?"

"Yes sir."

"But you don't agree with him do you?"

"I do not."

"Why not?"

"How could he know she was in the midst of changing rooms and was coming right back to that room?

"Well, for the sake of argument, let's say he was standing down by the desk, where he overheard the exchange between Ms. White and the desk clerk, and he waited to see her enter that second room and, shortly thereafter, leave and go up to retrieve her luggage from the first room. It's possible that could have happened, couldn't it?"

I was fleetingly tempted to answer "Standing down there in his black costume?" but that would have been a sarcastic answer to a legitimate question, as well as disrespectful to the dignity of the process, the court, and the jury, and I knew better. Instead, I said, "It's possible. Unlikely in my view, but, yes, possible, anything is possible."

He continued, "Possible. Thank you. Taking that further, because you say it's possible, I submit to you when she left the room and he knew she would return shortly, he used the lost master key and hid in the room awaiting her return."

I responded, "Using your hypothetical, where could he hide in the room and not be seen when she returned and, according to her testimony, turned on the lights?"

"Well, Mr. Sennewald, you're the security expert, not me. Where could he hide?"

"I've examined the room. Indeed, I measured the room. The only place a person could hide and not be seen when a guest enters would have to be in the bathroom to the right as you enter. The bathroom has an entry, not a door. The only place one could hide in that bathroom would be to stand in the bathtub, behind the shower curtain. The police detectives in this case are well-trained and experienced, even your expert acknowledges that. They're experienced criminal investigators, and they thought through where a culprit could hide and not be seen when someone entered the room. They knew the tub with the shower curtain was the only possible hiding place and they examined it for footprints. Their investigation, their examination, revealed no evidence of footprints in the bottom of that tub."

I was never asked if I had formed an opinion as to how the event occurred, but clearly rebutted Sonderman's theory and opinion. Apparently this left the jury with no positive expert support of Mary's version of the attack and no logical explanation for her bizarre story. I was excused and left the courtroom.

Following that concluding testimony, the next event is the closing arguments. I have no idea what the defense attorney had to say to the jury. I can only guess they somehow concluded the event did not happened as alleged, as I suspected, and they found for the hotel.

McCall v. Giant Stores

Contents

WHAT HAPPENED?

An employee, on her day off, returned a set of towels, a gift she had received from her mother after moving into her new apartment, to the store in which she worked. Upon presenting the merchandise for an exchange at the service desk, an older employee suspected her of stealing the merchandise and presenting it for an exchange. Challenged with this suspicion, she denied it and claimed she had just carried the merchandise into the store in one arm while she was carrying her baby in the other arm.

The suspicious employee immediately conducted a computer check of the database reflecting sales of specific inventory items, which indicated the items had never been purchased. A prompt search of videotapes covering the doors showed the now-suspect employee entering the store empty-handed. An untrained investigator came to the store several days later and interviewed the employee, who again denied any theft. The investigator called the police and the employee was subsequently jailed for theft.

WHO WAS BEING SUED, AND WHY?

A civil complaint was filed against Giant Stores for false imprisonment and wrongful termination caused by grossly careless, negligently managed, and untrained loss prevention employees who participated in the investigation and the plaintiff's questioning.

WHO WAS INVOLVED?

- Connie McCall, the employee who was accused of theft and was jailed.
- Barbara Schmidt, the service-desk employee who first suspected Connie.
- Pam Holdridge, the area supervisor who reported the theft to the regional loss prevention manager.
- Robert Greene, the in-store loss prevention agent who searched the videotapes and produced the videotape that depicted Connie entering the store empty-handed, the primary damning evidence.
- Mary Hinkley, the regional loss prevention manager who interrogated Connie, summoned the police, and requested the arrest of Connie based on the videotape evidence.
- Carl Whithers, the local police officer who transported Connie in handcuffs and incarcerated her in the local jail.
- Sandy Sanborne, the local criminal defense attorney retained by Connie to defend her in the criminal trial.
- Cindi Lang, the city attorney and prosecutor responsible for formalizing criminal complaints, initiating complaints in the local criminal justice system, and representing the state in criminal trials.
- Hildegarde McCall, Connie McCall's mother, who purchased the items believed to have been stolen.

WHEN DID IT HAPPEN?

Connie McCall returned a set of towels on a Saturday morning. The store personnel conducted their initial investigation that same morning.

Five days later Mary Hinkley, the investigator, arrived and interviewed Connie. That same day she reported her findings and the case to Officer Whithers. The next day, Whithers went to Connie's apartment and arrested her.

HOW DID IT HAPPEN?

I informed the calling attorney I was 99% retired and really wasn't interested in any further assignments, with the exception of a really "big-ticket" case that usually involved a wrongful death, catastrophic injury, or some other very egregious event. He promptly replied, "Then our case qualifies."

"How so?" I asked.

He went on to explain his firm represented a young female employee of a national retail firm who wrongfully accused her of theft and had her jailed based on a terribly flawed investigation. Indeed, the case was so badly handled by the retailer that this civil action was destined for punitive damages. So-called *punitive damages* means the court will allow the jury to punish a defendant for their conduct as a lesson not to repeat whatever the faulty conduct or failure to perform properly was. The vast percentage of awards that must be paid by a defendant are covered by insurance, however punitive awards must be paid out of the defendant's pocket, which can be painful.

"How was the store's investigation so terribly flawed?" I asked.

He mentioned that there were numerous failures and examples of investigative ineptitude, but the most egregious was the in-store security employee. In his haste to locate Connie entering the store, he seized on a section of the security videotape from the store's door, which showed her entering the store empty-handed at 10:10 a.m. Actually, she entered the store at 9:30 a.m., carrying the merchandise in one arm and her baby in the other. The store relied on the 10:10 a.m. scene in which the plaintiff was empty-handed and turned over that videotape to the police. It wasn't until just before the trial that the local prosecutor, while discussing the case with the defense attorney, sensed there was something wrong. The times on the videotapes are computer-generated and very difficult in some scenes to read, but following the 10:10 a.m. entry, that scene was spliced to the videotape from another camera viewing the service desk, and in that scene Connie was holding her baby!

But the scene with the baby was either ignored or the significance of the presence of the baby wasn't grasped. So the store concluded she entered carrying nothing, walked to the towel department, then carried the towels to the service desk and pretended they were hers. Yet the full (but spliced) videotape used as evidence revealed the presence of a baby in her arms. Where did the baby come from?

Subsequently, the store reexamined all the videotapes, upon the request of the city attorney, and in that search they found the section of videotape showing Connie entering the store at 9:30 a.m., carrying the package of towels and her baby and arriving within a minute at the service desk. Clearly, she was innocent of any theft and the store either intentionally spliced together scenes to support their theory or it was a gross act of negligence in not locating her initial entry, as she had contended.

The criminal charges that were before the court were dismissed "in the interest of justice." McCall then filed a civil suit against the store.

Her attorneys called me; we discussed some of the issues, as related above, and I accepted the case for two reasons: (1) to assist in hopes of ensuring Connie received just compensation for her treatment at the hands of a retailer that refused to raise the level of professionalism of the loss prevention/security personnel, something I have championed most of my adult life, and (2) for the satisfaction of engaging in and assisting in a punitive action case against a retailer who clearly doesn't understand, appreciate, or care about the importance of training its loss prevention staff, as proscribed in most of my books.

Interestingly, some years earlier a posting on a loss prevention Internet website stated, "I told my supervisor about Mr. Sennewald's book *Shoplifters vs. Retailers: The Rights of Both* and he cautioned me against reading it, saying, 'We don't care what Mr. Sennewald says; we do things the Giant Store way.'"

I was on board and the files started coming in.

DOCUMENTATION OF WHAT ACTUALLY TRANSPIRED

Connie entered the store through the east door at 9:30 a.m. carrying the set of towels her mother had given her for her new apartment. She didn't want to return them for a refund; she only wanted a different color to coordinate with her bathroom. In her other arm she was carrying her baby.

Procedure dictates when customers, including employees, enter the store carrying merchandise, typically for an exchange or a refund, the door "greeter" gives the customer a red slip and directs the customer to the service desk. This procedure is obviously incumbent upon the greeter to issue this colored slip; customers can't be expected to know the company's rules, however, employees know and should comply.

When Connie came in, the greeter was occupied and Connie didn't bother to go to her and request the slip. Instead, she walked directly to the service desk. Barbara Schmidt was one of the employees behind the desk; she recognized Connie and went to assist her. Connie placed the towel set on the counter and Barbara asked her for the red slip. Connie said the greeter was busy and she didn't get one, but would be happy to go back and get one if necessary. Barbara didn't believe the greeter was occupied and asked which door she had entered through. She then left the desk to verify Connie's story.

Barbara was suspicious Connie had entered the store without any merchandise, walked to the bed and bath department, picked up the towel set, and was presenting unpaid items for a refund. She even told her supervisor she had seen Connie approach the service desk from the area of the store where the bed and bath department was located. According to her sworn testimony in deposition, she was convinced Connie was dishonest and didn't think highly of her, mainly because Connie wore a small nose ring.

Connie sensed Barbara didn't believe her and words were exchanged. Connie called for a supervisor to come assist. Barbara got on the phone and called for Pam Holdridge, an area supervisor, to come to the service desk. While waiting for Pam, Barbara knew the code to access the inventory site that reflects current levels of inventory by classification number, and that site also reflected recent sales of each item. When Pam arrived, Barbara told her of her suspicion, and confirmed it with the information from the inventory site that showed no sales within the last month of the items Connie was bringing back. Now Pam was convinced Connie stole the items, but she knew better than to call her a liar, so she instructed Connie to go the department and select the colors she wanted.

Connie, still carrying her baby, did just that, and Pam issued her a small credit for the difference in the price, which accomplished what Connie had come for and the matter was concluded. That is, concluded in Connie's mind, but not Pam Holdridge's, who immediately phoned the company's regional loss prevention manager, Mary Hinkley, and informed her of what had transpired.

Mary, in turn, phoned the store's loss prevention agent, Robert Greene, and gave him an overview of the event and the employees' suspicions. She directed him to go to the camera room and review the videotapes of both doors that morning to verify the suspicion that she entered without the goods. She also instructed him to check all the cameras that would capture the image of the route from both doors to the bed and bath department in hopes of actually catching Connie in the theft on videotape.

Later, Robert admitted he was upset with this task because it takes a lot of time to patiently review all the footage. He didn't mind the work so much as the time it took, because his performance evaluation was only on the number of shoplifters he caught each month, and any task that took him away from shoplifting detection invariably impacted his review. The review affected his salary increases and opportunities for promotion. So, he reluctantly rushed through the search for Connie entering the store, and, fortunately, he found her coming in at 10:10 a.m. He couldn't find her walking to or from the bed and bath area, but the quality of videos on the old equipment was such that it could be missed easily. He reported his findings to Mary. Mary then asked him to check the work schedule and inform her as to when Connie was due to work again. He complied. It was in the next week.

Mary arrived at the store five days later, while Connie was on shift, and briefly met with Barbara who, again, stated she checked the inventory base and the goods hadn't been sold; she talked with Pam who restated Barbara's suspicions as to what Connie had done; and she met with Robert and viewed the spliced videotape. As Robert had reported, the computer-generated time-of-day reflected Connie entering the east door at 10:10 a.m. empty-handed and then a vague image of Connie with a baby in her arms at the service desk, but the time was difficult to read.

Convinced the entry image was the proof Connie was lying, Mary called Connie in from the floor and met with her at one of the store's executive offices. A clerk sat behind Connie, taking notes on a notebook. Mary introduced herself, then broached the issue with the importance of always telling the truth, and stated she could be helpful to those employees who might have made a mistake. She then asked Connie to tell her about the towel set.

Connie said she had moved into a new apartment and her mom gave her the towels as a gift, but the colors clashed with the walls and she wanted to exchange them. She knew her mother purchased the towels in this store, so she brought them back to exchange for the right color and "everyone jumped my case, like I took 'em or something."

"Well, that's not the evidence that I have. I have it all on video," said Mary.

"Let me see it, and I can explain it."

"I'm not going to show you my evidence. You tell me what happened," said Mary.

"I told you already. If you don't believe me, call my mom. Please, call my mom and she'll tell you."

"I don't have to call your mom. I have the tape. ... Okay," said Mary, "if you don't want to tell me, I want you to sit in this office and write out for me what happened. Will you do that?"

While Connie sat in the office alone she wrote out a brief statement, reiterating what she had said earlier, signed it, and then, upset with the confrontation and accusation, left the store, essentially walking off the job.

While Connie was in the office writing her statement, Mary phoned the local police department and requested an officer come to the store and transport a prisoner.

By the time Officer Withers arrived, Connie had already left. Mary informed Withers of the offense committed by Connie and their investigative efforts, then provided a copy of the spliced videotape. Withers left after writing his report and took the videotape as evidence.

When the officer left, Mary wrote her concluding investigative employee report and, interestingly, included the total retail value of the original towel set as "full restitution." The significance of this is it clearly indicates a recovery of the amount (e.g., $37.00), similar to a shoplifting case when the culprit is captured along with the merchandise, and the goods have been recovered and are back in inventory—another form of quantitative measurements justifying the security program.

The next day when Withers determined Connie was not in the store working, he went in the early evening hours to her apartment. He knocked, announcing his presence and his need to see Connie. Connie ran up the stairs and quickly phoned her mother. Her mother told her to let him in and cooperate; she had nothing to worry about.

Withers arrested her and informed her she was going to the station for booking. She asked about her baby, asleep upstairs. "Get someone here quick. I don't have time to wait for babysitters." Half panicking, Connie called her mother again, who dropped everything and came to the apartment.

At the station, Withers sat Connie down and asked her to tell him the truth. She said she had told everyone the truth. He gave up and placed her in a cell. As she cried, another officer came in and tried to calm her and, as they talked, she said they wouldn't even let her see the video. He got the videotape and let her see it, and she saw immediately that the video reflected her second entry into the store that day. The officer didn't understand that or its significance, but at least she knew that the store had provided bad evidence and she knew what direction to take when she could talk to an attorney.

Once released from jail, Connie sought out an attorney. She explained to her attorney, Sandy Sanborne, how she ran into her dad in the store after she exchanged the towels and they talked a few minutes. He told Connie that her sister was out in his truck, and she should go see her. She left the store with the new towels and the baby, found her sister, and they visited for a few minutes. Then she remembered she wanted to purchase a small item. She asked her sister to take the baby and said she'd be right back. She reentered the store at 10:10 a.m. and left five minutes later.

Armed with this information and after viewing the video evidence, Sandy made an appointment with the city attorney, Cindi Lang, and they both viewed the video. An enhancement of that spliced section following her entry into the store indicated the time was 9:32 a.m. It was evident she couldn't enter at 10:10 a.m. and be at the service desk at 9:32 a.m.

Because of that error, the computerized inventory site was obtained and a careful inspection revealed that indeed the very towel set that Connie had brought into the store was sold some days earlier. Barbara, in her haste, missed that entry and misled her supervisor. Barbara's results of the database search were never verified by Pam, Robert, or, more importantly, Mary.

In my evaluation I was provided with 46 different records, policies, transcripts, files, and videos. Among the materials, I could not find a company/corporate policy on how to handle investigations involving suspected employees. To this day I do not know if the defendant simply defied the court and hid that policy (in the language of the industry, "hiding the ball") out of fear it would be catastrophic if I saw it and would show the jury how they failed to follow their own directives, or if indeed they were operating without one. Either way, it's a classic case of unprofessionalism, negligence, and, no matter how you slice it, anti-employee.

Just one of five very simple actions could have derailed this tragic event:

1. Assuming the splicing of the wrong time was carelessness and not intentional, any careful inspection of the video given to the police could have noted the time differential, which would have sent everyone back to the drawing boards.
2. If Mary had but an iota of curiosity about how the baby could be in Connie's arms *after* she entered empty-handed, the truth of the employee's version would have surfaced.
3. If Mary had taken the time to check the inventory database for past sales, rather than relying on a service desk clerk (who apparently had an ax to grind), a more careful examination of the facts would have occurred; Barbara's information would have been refuted, and the truth of an earlier sale would have given a different direction to the investigation.
4. If Mary allowed Connie to view the video in that executive office, it would have shed an entirely new light on their suspicions and beliefs.
5. If Mary called Connie's mother it most likely would have thrown a new light on the question, worth exploring.

THE TRIAL

On the day of my appearance on the witness stand I was informed the thrust of the defense was going to be the whole matter was Connie's fault for failing to follow the well-known company rule that merchandise being brought back into a store had to be checked by the door greeter.

In a civil trial the plaintiff goes first—that is, they are the first to present their case. Various witnesses were called, including Connie's mother, Hildegarde McCall, who testified she purchased the towel set and produced the receipt. When I took the stand, on direct examination, I testified as to my opinions, which I had written out for counsel, and were essentially as follows:

- The organizational structure of Giant Store's security program does not include or allow for trained and professional district-level investigators, who are common in large store chains. Instead, they required district loss prevention managers to assume that important responsibility, along with a myriad of other supervisorial and inspectional tasks related to all the stores in their district (five in this case).

- Investigations into alleged or suspected internal dishonesty are typically time consuming and require aptitude, in-depth experience, and investigative training. Mary did not have the time, aptitude, experience, or proper training.

- There is conflicting information about specific policies and procedures relative to internal investigations. Apparently there was no written policy and procedure in place to guide Mary. Failure to have a policy and procedure in accusing and referring employees to the police for criminal prosecution is unthinkable and falls below the industry's custom and practice.

- The ineptitude of the investigation was staggering—from the hastily patched videotape scenes, to the inclusion of nonsecurity personnel to do the computer search for any record of the purchase, to the failure to grasp the enormity of the fact the employee appeared with the towels and a baby in her arms and no one asked how the child got there, coupled with the absolute refusal to investigate further when the employee refused to confess—and resulted in an egregious injustice to a fellow employee.

- Mary, without written guidelines, without approval, without guidance from her supervisor, and without human resources or store management oversight, acted unilaterally against Connie. Referring an employee of the company to the police without some objective management agreement or approval is contrary to and below the standard of care of most businesses and industry, let alone the retail industry.

- Once this wrongful accusation, arrest, and attempted prosecution of an employee became known to the company, no level of upper management felt the need to investigate what and how it happened nor correct or purge the records memorializing this alleged crime by an employee. In fact, Connie's supervisor never even read the report of the incident until just prior to her disposition, almost a year later. And that supervisor defends Mary's handling of the investigation suggesting it was Connie's fault for not getting the red sticker when she entered the store. Any responsible employer would discipline Mary, counsel her supervisor, and expunge any records that reflect Connie's guilt.
- The store's CCTV system in place at the time was worn and outdated and the images, in some cases, were of such poor quality that it contributed to this mishandled investigation.

I don't recall the exact question put to me by my client, Connie's attorney, but I do recall my answer, telling the jury the following: "I couldn't sleep last night thinking about the matter of no written policy for the handling of employee investigations, and it finally dawned on me: the company has very clear and detailed policies and procedures on how to handle shoplifting cases, but no clear and detailed policies or procedures for investigations involving suspected employees? Why? The answer is the company is afraid of customers if the store makes a mistake, but they're not afraid of employees because if they make a mistake they can claim employee misconduct and get rid of the employee, so more latitude is available if not proscribed by strict guidelines."

Cross-examination, which follows the direct examination, is usually aggressive, but the attorney representing the store, a gentleman and quality lawyer, apparently felt the weight of evidence against his client was such that it would bear little or no fruit to challenge me. He did ask the following: "Now Mr. Sennewald, you'd agree, would you not, that stores must have rules?"

"Yes, I agree."

"Indeed, you've recommended the implementation of various rules for employees, haven't you?"

"Yes sir," I replied.

"And to operate an orderly store or business every employee must comply with the rules, you'd agree with that, would you not?"

"Yes."

"And you've testified you know Ms. McCall broke the store's rules, did you not?"

My response, "I did. Yes, she broke the rules, and in my view the store has every right to enforce their rules and demand compliance. Ms. McCall should have been disciplined for breaking the rules. She should not have been put in jail for a crime she didn't commit."

That concluded my testimony. I was excused by the court, left the courtroom, and returned to my home in California. It was the last trial of my long career.

The store did not offer any witness or testimony in their defense. The matter, as I understand it, settled that very afternoon.

CHAPTER 10

A Summarization of Cases Based on the Theory of Liability, False Arrest/False Imprisonment, or Excessive Use of Force

Contents

FARATOOM v. CITY UNIVERSITY

The plaintiff, Karim Faratoom, is an employee of the university and manager of the central computer system. He arrives late one morning due to traffic congestion and parks illegally in front of the academic building housing the central computer network. The computer network must be up and running for the entire academic community at 7:00 a.m. and it's now 7:10 a.m.

He runs in, activates the system, and runs out only to find a campus policeman has just finished immobilizing his vehicle with a Rhino Boot, a heavy metal device attached to one wheel that prevents a driver from moving his or her vehicle. Karim, in his anger and frustration, kicks the Rhino Boot; words are exchanged, an argument ensues, and the campus officer wrestles Karim to the ground and handcuffs him. In the process, Karim's shoulder is injured. Karim is arrested and transported to the city jail. The matter is later dismissed in the municipal court. A civil action was filed against the university and officer on the grounds of false arrest, false imprisonment, and excessive use of force.

The plaintiff counsel's research identified me as an experienced campus police administrator, called me, and we discussed the case on the phone. After he explained the incident, he asked if I would assist as his expert. I agreed and was retained by counsel for the plaintiff.

During the trial, I testified on direct examination Karim should never have been arrested and jailed. The issuance of a parking citation would have been warranted, but the officer went too far and had no grounds to handcuff and arrest the plaintiff.

On cross-examination the attorney for the university asked if I believed people should be arrested if they committed crimes, as a general proposition.

"Yes, of course," I answered.

"Then why are you telling the jury Mr. Faratoom should not have been arrested?"

"Because he didn't commit a crime, he committed a parking infraction."

"He most certainly did commit a crime sir," responded the attorney. "He committed the crime of vandalism and destruction of property by kicking the university's equipment."

I partially rose from the witness chair on the stand, leaned over the rail, and while pointing at the very Rhino Boot that had been brought in as evidence and was lying on the floor in front of the jury, stated, "The arrest report reflects Mr. Faratoom was wearing tennis shoes when booked into the city jail. I submit to you, a man could kick that 50-pound iron device all day while wearing tennis shoes and not even scratch it, let alone destroy it. He did not vandalize or destroy any property, and he should never have been physically put on the ground, should not have been arrested, and certainly should never have been jailed."

All eyes were fixed on the iron Rhino Boot.

The jury found for the plaintiff, who was subsequently compensated by the university.

JAMES v. QUICKWAY MARKETS

Elmer James, an elderly resident of a retirement home, walked three blocks to the store for cigarettes early one morning. Only one register was open and no other customers were there. He approached the cashier from the main aisle that runs parallel to the front of the store, informing him he wanted a pack of Pall Mall cigarettes.

Cigarettes were no longer displayed behind the cashier as in times past. The cashier knew the price of one pack, accepted the money, and gave Elmer change and the receipt. The two briefly exchanged small talk, and the cashier directed Elmer to the newly installed plastic cigarette cases along the front end of the grocery store.

"Just get your Pall Mall's from the case, Mr. James."

Elmer walked away from the register toward the cigarette cases and, at that very moment, a store security agent entered the store behind Elmer and noticed him walking toward the other set of entrance doors. The cigarette cases were to Elmer's left. The agent saw Elmer stop, approach the cases, lift the plastic door, remove a pack of cigarettes, place the package in his shirt pocket, and continue out of the store. The agent believed he had just witnessed an act of shoplifting.

Arrests for shoplifting require six steps (conditions):

1. The agent must see the customer approach the merchandise.
2. The agent must see the customer select the merchandise.
3. The agent must see where the merchandise is concealed.
4. The agent must maintain uninterrupted surveillance of the customer to ensure the stolen merchandise isn't "dumped" or disposed of.
5. The shoplifter must pass all registers where the goods could be purchased.
6. The agent should stop (make contact with) the shoplifter outside the store.

The agent, satisfied he had a shoplifting situation, followed Elmer outside, interrupted his progress, and asked him to surrender the package of cigarettes. Elmer had a hearing problem and, startled by the thought this stranger was trying to rob him of the cigarettes, he refused and abruptly turned away while reaching in his pocket. He was thrown to the ground. Later it was discovered that the fall to the ground broke two of Elmer's ribs.

While being escorted back into the store, the sole cashier recognized Elmer and asked what was happening. When told, the cashier informed security Elmer had indeed purchased the pack and had been told to go select his brand from the display case.

In this case, two defendants were named in the lawsuit, the store and a security firm that provided security agents. I was retained by both defense firms. During the pretrial deposition and while under oath, I was asked if I faulted either defendant. I did. I testified I faulted the store for selling an item when the merchandise wasn't at the register, for sending the customer to fetch his purchase after the transaction, and for failing to keep the plastic cases containing cigarettes locked at all times, as specifically required by the municipal code. Those failures greatly contributed to the event. The store's attorney (my attorney) cringed, but he knew this was coming; it simply meant I sank the store, my own "client."

With respect to the other defendant, the security firm providing the security agent, I testified I did not fault the actions of the agent, including the use of force, because there was evidence Elmer attempted to pull a knife from his pocket to defend himself, and the agent was acting in self-defense. Further, the agent, following the industry standards and based on his observations, believed he was lawfully engaged in overcoming resistance by a person who had just committed a crime.

The matter settled without going to trial.

GARCIA v. GRAND LION HOTEL AND CASINO

Leon Garcia was a recovering alcoholic, but convinced his wife a weekend at the high-end Grand Lion Hotel and Casino would be an appropriate celebration for their anniversary, and he promised not to drink. While at the gaming tables, he did drink and got drunk. Leon was considered a "high-roller" because of his large wagers. Mrs. Garcia had to pull her husband away from the blackjack table to go get something to eat. She knew food would help him sober up. They were comped a free meal to the nicest steak house in the hotel.

During the meal, Leon ordered and drank wine. In his state of intoxication he became loud and obnoxious, including crunching on and swallowing escargot shells, which was so revolting that customers were leaving and refusing to pay for their meals. The maître'd and waiters were unable to quiet Leon, so security was called and two plainclothes security supervisors responded.

Mrs. Garcia, equally disgusted with her husband, left and went to their room, commenting as she departed, "He's your problem now."

Leon was seated in the middle of a half-moon-shaped booth. With loud profanities he refused to listen to or comply with the security officers. They decided to pull the table out so they could seize him and escort him out of the restaurant and to his room, a common courtesy extended to guests. However, the table was anchored to the floor and they couldn't pull it out to reach him. Shortly, a waiter walked by carrying a bottle of wine; Leon thought it was his order and scooted out to chase down the waiter. Instead, he ended up in the hands of the security officers. Leon would not cooperate, and, eventually, force was required to remove him from the restaurant. In that process he violently resisted, and the ensuing struggle took all three to the floor and he was handcuffed. He was escorted to a service elevator, taken to the security office, and placed in a security holding room used for detainees pending arrival of the police. In the room, because of his violence, the cuffs were left on.

The holding room was constantly monitored by a CCTV camera. Officers watched him refuse to sit on the chair. Leon laid and rolled on the floor, moaning and complaining he was in pain. Local police responded and observed Leon in his drunken state, and instructed the security officers to keep Leon handcuffed until a police transportation van could swing by and take him to jail. Mrs. Garcia phoned the security office to determine what was happing. She was asked to come to the security office and calm down her husband and take him to their room. She refused. They informed her they were willing to bring him up to the room but she said she didn't want him in his drunken state. They said he could end up in jail. She stated, "So be it," and informed them to be cautious because he was a diabetic.

In an abundance of caution, paramedics were called. Before they arrived, Leon said his chest hurt. Paramedics arrived, checked him, and asked him about the pains, which he said were no longer present. The paramedics left. Police eventually returned and took him to the city jail.

Mrs. Garcia arrived in the morning, arranged for a bail bond, and Leon was released. Once outside, he started vomiting blood. Mrs. Garcia took him to the nearest hospital, where it was determined he was experiencing a serious heart attack. Eventually he had a heart transplant, following a massive heart failure.

The Garcias sued the hotel for falsely arresting him, using force to arrest him, for keeping him in handcuffs while in the small detention room, and for not providing him with prompt medical care.

I served as the hotel's expert witness and testified that the security officers' conduct was in keeping with custom and practice in the industry, that each act was in appropriate response to the situation, and the entire event was in direct response to Leon's unreasonable state of intoxication. I told them I had spent hours watching the CCTV monitor looking for any act or conduct by the officers that was unreasonable or even disrespectful and found none.

Interestingly, the jury concluded the security officers' conduct was proper but, nonetheless, awarded a substantial amount of money to Leon because of his huge expenses for a heart transplant. The law does not allow that. A defendant cannot be required to pay compensation unless that defendant is responsible for the damages. The hotel was not liable, and therefore there was a mistrial. A new trial was set.

Two years later the entire case was retried before a different jury, this time in the U.S. federal court, and the jury found for the hotel.

HICKHAM v. THE MUNICIPAL ZOO

Three young men had been celebrating and drinking beer all night. Just before daylight they decided to go to the park next to the zoo, climb one of the huge trees there, and watch the sunrise.

While up in the tree they made loud monkey sounds, frightening the gazelles in a pen adjacent to the zoo's perimeter. The gazelles, in the immediate vicinity of the row of trees, became alarmed and, in a crazed frenzy, started running and jumping, risking injury to themselves and each other. Their keeper, also alarmed, called the zoo's security office, reporting someone in the trees along the edge of the zoo was creating loud sounds and frightening the animals in his area. Security arrived in the general area and, while waiting quietly, identified the location of the tree, among all the trees, by the noise the men were making. The armed security officer noted the plastic cups with beer sitting around the base of the tree, looked up, and saw the men. The officer shouted for them to come down. Two came down without incident, but the third, Bobby Hickham, lost his footing and fell, landing on the tree's exposed root system, causing lifelong paralysis. He sued the zoo claiming the armed officer's fierce shouting was menacing, causing great fear, and because he was frightened he lost his footing. The plaintiff's primary criticism was the presence of the officer's gun, claiming that if the officer had not been armed, Bobby wouldn't have been so fearful and could have maintained his composure. The gun, coupled with the stern vocal command by the security officer, was a form of excessive use of force.

I was the zoo's security expert witness. I visited the site, measured the distance from the ground to the branch on which the defendant was seated while holding his beer, and inspected the appearance of the security officer in question. I shared with the court that, in my opinion, there was nothing untoward about the officer or his appearance with the weapon in its holster, and stated that because of the distance up in the tree, the officer had no option but to shout to be heard, especially to be heard over the noise these three intoxicated men were making.

Every trial is either a court trial or a jury trial. This matter was a court trial because the plaintiff had waived his rights to a trial by jury. The judge ruled in favor of the zoo.

JOHNSON v. DANDY MARKETS

Dandy Markets' assistant store manager, Gene Fillmore, was seated in his car in the parking lot in front of the store, eating his lunch. The market was the anchor store in a relatively small strip shopping center that contained a beauty salon, dry cleaners, real estate office, shoe repair shop, camera shop, and liquor store. The market also sold liquor. The market was on the east end of the row of stores, and the liquor store anchored the west end.

As Gene comfortably lounged in the front seat, listening to his car radio with a sandwich in hand, he observed a black man walking east-bound directly in front of the market carrying four gallons of whiskey, of different sorts, two on each shoulder. His fingers were gripping the glass handles on the large bottles' necks.

Gene had not observed this man exit the market through its western-most doors, so he didn't know if the man had even been in his store or not, but there was no question in his mind he was witnessing a shoplifting incident. He immediately jumped out of his car and shouted at the man to stop. Gene testified he had every intention of arresting the man for the theft of the whiskey, despite the fact he hadn't observed a theft. The mere presence of the man and whiskey being carried in this unusual fashion told the experienced grocery manager the culprit had simply snatched the bottles from the display shelf and walked right out the door.

Gus Johnson, the man with the whiskey, was startled by Gene shout-ing in the parking lot. He dropped the four bottles on the sidewalk, all breaking, and commenced running eastbound. He turned at the corner of the store with Gene in pursuit. The store's receiving dock was located on that side of the store. A tractor and trailer were backed up to the dock and several store employees were sitting on the dock eating their lunch. The young employees on the dock were startled to see Johnson running toward them with Gene in hot pursuit, so they jumped to the ground to assist the store manager. Gus was clearly trapped, so he dove under the trailer. A number of legs were sticking out on both sides of the trailer as the men grappled with Gus and finally pulled him out and got him up on his feet. Gus started screaming, "That was my whiskey and you scared me and made me drop 'em," all the while tugging and trying to twist free.

Gene shouted for one of the dock employees to call the police while the other employees got Gus up onto the dock and took him to a bale of used cardboard, by the bailer, and laid him face down. Three of the men laid on Gus to keep him pinned down pending the arrival of the police.

The police arrived in a relatively short period of time and promptly ordered the men off of their prisoner. Gus didn't move; he was dead. He had died of positional asphyxia, starved of oxygen because of the weight of the employees on his back.

I was retained by the law firm representing Gus Johnson's survivors. In my view the excessive use of force theory of liability was a "no brainer."

For three husky, healthy young men to lie on a 50-year-old man of thin stature was unnecessary and excessive. Indeed, such weight on any man or woman would produce the same results—asphyxia.

The store attempted to mitigate their liability with the position they were trying to restrain a shoplifter, and even if they hadn't witnessed the actual crime, the circumstances of the event provided sufficient probable cause he had stolen the whiskey and any prudent man would have reacted as did the store.

But did Johnson steal the whiskey from the Dandy Market? My examination of the facts, almost a year after the event, revealed the broken bottles were never recovered; the bar codes were never scanned; no inventory was taken that day that could have reflected a shortage or no shortage; no cashiers were interviewed as to their knowledge of a sale; no register tapes were examined in an effort to locate a sale; and no effort was made to determine if the store at the end of the mall had any losses, sales, or memory of Gus Johnson.

True, no security agent was on duty in that store that day, but a loss prevention investigator should have been dispatched from the corporate offices to piece together a clearer picture. That wasn't done.

The general rule in the retail industry is if you didn't see it, it didn't happen. Indeed, there are six steps that serve as guidelines for shoplifting detections, as outlined earlier in this chapter.

The jury concluded no crime could be established, consequently the detention of Gus Johnson was unlawful and the method of restraining him was unnecessary, unlawful, and excessive use of force. The Johnsons' suit prevailed and the family was compensated.

WASHINGTON v. CLOUSE AND FINE'S DEPARTMENT STORES

Following church, Sonjia Washington and her mother, father, and two little brothers went to Fine's to exchange a dress. They were followed by a close family friend driving her own car. The women made the exchange on the main floor of the store while Mr. Washington and the two boys rode the escalator downstairs. Following the exchange, Sonjia, her mother, and the family friend browsed the various departments on that main floor. In the normal course of events, Sonjia was picked up by a security camera as she approached the costume jewelry department, a historically high-theft area. The camera was being monitored by loss prevention agent

Becky Schmidt. Schmidt observed Sonjia select an inexpensive, expandable bracelet with colored stones and slip it on her left wrist. Sonjia then left the department wearing the bracelet and located her mother. Schmidt could see the nine-year-old girl showing her mother the bracelet. Mrs. Washington appeared to look at her daughter's wrist and then went about her shopping. It was apparent there was a brief discussion between the two of them.

Sonjia returned to the jewelry department and looked at other items, but did not remove or return the bracelet to its former display fixture. She left that area still wearing the item and joined the family friend, browsing through other goods.

Mr. Washington and the boys returned to the main floor about the time Schmidt radioed her partner, Jeanie Custer, and informed her she had what appeared was going to be a shoplifting incident. Schmidt requested Custer stand by the parking lot exit doors for possible assistance if needed. Three male loss prevention agents also working in the store heard Schmidt's call on their radios, and, although not requested to assist, decided they too would stand by in the area of the exit, just in case.

The Washington family briefly met; the father and two boys immediately left the store and headed for the family car, parked about seven parking spaces out in the lot once you crossed the rather wide driveway that separated the sidewalk and stores from the lot. Mr. Washington had no knowledge of his daughter wearing a bracelet belonging to the store.

The ladies, including Sonjia, followed, but walked much slower, engaging in conversation as they crossed the wide driveway. Midway across that driveway, they were confronted by Schmidt, who had left her monitoring station and came to the main floor to deal with the problem. She interrupted the ladies conversation by saying, "Excuse me, ma'am (addressing Mrs. Washington), but your daughter is wearing a bracelet she didn't pay for."

The mother turned to her daughter and in a loud voice said, "What in the world are you doing with this? This ain't yours. Shame on you," and she pulled the bracelet from her daughter's wrist. Mrs. Washington started to hand it to Schmidt, but it fell on the pavement.

As this moment, Mr. Washington had just put the two boys in the back seat of the car and got in the driver's seat. He heard, or thought he heard, his wife's raised voice.

Custer was standing behind Schmidt when Schmidt informed Mrs. Washington, "I'm sorry ma'am, but your daughter will have to return to the store with us," to which the mother, now louder than before replied, "What for? You all got your bracelet, you know my name because of the purchases I made, and you ain't taking my daughter nowhere!"

Mr. Washington couldn't help but hear his wife now and, alarmed, started to get out of the car to go investigate what was going on.

The three male agents, more or less "hovering" in the background and watching this event unfold, had moved close to the Washington's car and, seeing the father starting to head back to where the "arrest" was being made, blocked Mr. Washington's path, asking him, "Where do you think you're going?"

By now Schmidt had grabbed Sonjia's arm to escort her to the store and Mrs. Washington, a large woman, pushed Schmidt away from her daughter. Custer stepped in and she also got pushed away by Mrs. Washington, who now was shouting for them to get away from her and her daughter.

Mr. Washington, with no idea as to the nature of the trouble, and intent on getting to his wife and daughter, attempted to push through the three men blocking his way and a scuffle ensued, resulting in all four men going to the ground. Mr. Washington struggled to get the men off him and to respond to the continued shouting some 80 feet away. One of the loss prevention agents got Mr. Washington into a chokehold around his neck and the other two continued to lay on top of him to immobilize him so he couldn't get up.

The shopping center security and police responded to the scene based on a radio call for help from Schmidt. Customers were now gathering around to watch the event.

The first police officer on the scene found the pile of men. One of the loss prevention agents said their "suspect" was "playing possum." The officer instructed them to let loose and get up. Mr. Washington was not conscious. Paramedics were summoned. Mouth-to-mouth resuscitation failed to bring Mr. Washington around, and he was pronounced dead upon arrival at the hospital. The coroner's report reflected Mr. Washington had died as a result of asphyxiation.

A summarization of the event would be as follows: the plaintiff's (Mrs. Washington) nine-year-old daughter shoplifted without the knowledge of her parents. Store detectives stopped the girl while walking with her mother out to the car in the lot. The father had walked ahead and wasn't present when the mother and girl were stopped. He heard the commotion and started to return. Mr. Washington was intercepted by three more store agents. He struggled and was choked to death.

I was retained by counsel representing the surviving family and testified in deposition as to my opinions, which were critical of the store, including:

1. The entire event could have been prevented by a simple phone call from Schmidt to any employee in the area, who could have mentioned the bracelet to either the little girl or her mother before they left.

2. The "theft" wasn't prevented because an arrest was the sole quantitative measurement of performance of store loss prevention agents—that is, "prevention" didn't count, and Schmidt was below her quota for the month.

3. Insisting the girl return to the store inflamed an already potentially volatile confrontation. Besides, when a child is caught shoplifting, the practice in the industry is to simply call and inform the parent. In this case, the parent was informed right on the scene. This is not a matter that would be referred to the police or juvenile authorities. There was no need to require the child to return to the store. All necessary information was available because of the mother's earlier transaction.

4. The deployment of five professional security agents to deal with the theft of a child's bracelet was a reflection of poor judgment on the part of all agents involved as well as their supervision and training. It simply fell below custom and practice.

5. The three male agents had no legal grounds to intercept or use any force on Mr. Washington. He had committed no crime, nor was he even aware that a crime may have been committed.

6. The force that was used reflected these agents had not been properly trained in the use of force.

The matter settled prior to trial.

CHAPTER 11

A Summarization of Cases Predicated on Negligence as the Theory of Liability

Contents

MILLER v. JASON CARTWRIGHT AND GREATER LEGION HALL

Mildred Miller was the owner of Old Lace Antique Jewelry, a well-known boutique specializing in purchasing and selling antique jewelry in the historic part of town. Her store was professionally surveyed and designed to protect her inventory with state-of-the-art security hardware; a customer couldn't just open the door and walk directly into her shop. Visitors were required to ring a bell, and Mildred or her sister would buzz open the door if they recognized the person or the customer looked "legitimate." If the visitor did not appear trustworthy, they wouldn't open the door. If the sisters absolutely didn't like the potential customer for any reason, including anything from grooming to ethnicity, they simply would say, "Sorry, we're closing for inventory," and close temporarily.

The high point for Mildred's business each year was the antique and jewelry show held in the Greater Legion Hall. Sellers had to pay a fee to show their inventory; the size of the fee was in relation to the size of the show space (i.e., "booth"). Jason Cartwright was the promoter of the annual event and coordinated everything from publicity, advertising, assignment of selling spaces, special needs, and security during the event. Typically there were over 200 different vendors with their exhibits in the sales area.

Mildred and Jason had known each other for years. He wasn't an antique dealer, but he went around the country promoting antique shows as a unique and specialized business. By virtue of that long connection with the trade, he was quite accustomed to eccentric, cranky, or cagey shopkeepers.

Mildred always insisted on the very center of the hall, the largest selling space. She placed her lockable showcases in a large square and during the three-day event she, her sister, and two nieces (who were learning the business) manned the booth. Because she was wary and ever-alert, her business had never lost as much as a costume jewelry ring.

This year, she had various pieces on display, and according to her, the value exceeded $750,000 at retail prices. No one knew the real value.

Jason's security plan this year was the same as the years prior. During the hours the show was open, armed guards were stationed at the two main entrances, and a guard was posted at the vendor's door by the kitchen area. The officers were equipped with two-way radios and Jason assumed the role of chief of security. The contractual understanding was the protection of merchandise was the sole responsibility of the vendors and the presence (and costs) of the uniformed officers was simply to provide a security presence and action in the event of an emergency.

Every door, including emergency exits, was alarmed. All the windows were protected with breaking-glass sensors (electronic devices that hear and react to the unique sound of breaking glass). The alarm system also included two "panic buttons," smoke sensors, and water-flow sensors.

When the show closed each evening, the vendors locked their goods in the cases and took home exceptionally valuable pieces. Once the public vacated the building the doors were all locked and chained. Three guards remained on duty, two wandering the floor (more or less overseeing the lockdown by each merchant) and one manned the vendor door (overseeing the departing workers). Once the building was confirmed empty of all customers and vendors, the three guards were relieved by the night guard, who chained himself in by roping the chain around and over the doors panic hardware. Lights were turned off except for scattered low-illumination bulbs to allow the interior guard to make his hourly rounds.

On the morning of the last day of the show, the vendors filtered in and went to their respective booths to prepare for the day. When the Miller sisters and one niece walked to their area, Mildred screamed and fainted. Her cases had been opened and most of her inventory was simply gone! Jason was in the building and he ran to the scene, then quickly radioed for the police and instructed the security guards to seal the building so no one else could come in or leave. Within a matter of minutes, the vendor of a neighboring booth shouted and pointed to a rope dangling through an opening in the ceiling.

Investigation revealed there was a modified penthouse-like structure on the roof of the great hall that housed air-conditioning units. The access doors of that structure were not alarmed nor were they equipped with locks. The burglars, either current employees, ex-employees, or professional burglars with contacts with the hall or with the air-conditioning service company, entered the penthouse and carefully removed some of the wood flooring. Looking through that opening one could see the upper side of the suspended ceiling tiles. It was then a simple matter to remove some of the ceiling tiles, tie a rope, and lower themselves down (and pull themselves up) the rope dangling down into the center of the hall. Other ropes left behind in the penthouse indicated they were used to pull up baskets of goods for eventual removal from the property. Inspection of the exterior of the building revealed physical evidence as to where and how the building was scaled.

The interior guard, who was allowed to sit in the kitchen office and watch television between patrols, never heard a sound, and when he made his regular rounds he saw nothing suspicious. Mildred was financially wiped out and several other merchants sustained significant losses. The police never solved the crime.

Mildred filed a lawsuit against the promoter and owner of the Greater Legion Hall claiming they were negligent in their obligation to protect her property.

The plaintiff's expert opined the guard should never have been allowed to watch TV and should have been continually patrolling instead. I served as the defendant's expert and testified the security measures were reasonable and adequate, but were defeated by a professional criminal plan that even confounded the police.

I countered the plaintiff's expert with my opinion of the security measures in place, and, considering the relatively small area (albeit it was a large enclosed hall), constant walking would have been an unreasonable requirement of a security officer. I further stated no security executive or professional consultant would have recommended or required a guard to constantly patrol such a relatively small space, which was already secured with chained doors. In view of the strategy of chaining the doors, I considered the guard's presence more of a fire watch than a crime prevention assignment. In my opinion, there was no negligence in the protective strategy for the event, including no negligence in the absence of alarms or locks on the penthouse because of the unforeseeability of a professional criminal attack in that kind of building.

The jury found there was no negligence, therefore the Greater Legion Hall was not liable for the loss.

BROWN v. ACE ALARM COMPANY

Benny's Place was a typical local bar tucked back in a zone between very modest homes, commercial buildings, and the railroad yards. As a rule, only locals patronized the bar. A new face or stranger would be hard-pressed to linger after one bottle of beer. It was almost like a private club or family.

Hal Brown was a brakeman for the railroad, and when he was in town he could be found at Benny's. Hal, for his own safety while working in the railroads switching yards at night, carried a small automatic pistol in his overalls and had done so for years. Some people knew it, some probably didn't.

On the fateful night of November 14 the bar was jumping. The jukebox never stopped; if it did Margie Trimm, the bartender, put in more quarters. The little bumper-pool table was busy and the smoke hung heavy halfway down from the ceiling. It was, as always, noisy with chatter and laughter.

As is typical, the clock on the wall was 20 minutes fast. As the hour of 2:00 a.m. approached, Margie called out "Last call!" At about 1:55 a.m., bar time, only Margie, Hal, and three other patrons were still there. Margie approached the door to lock it when she was violently forced back in by two men in masks rushing in, each carrying a handgun. The assailants shouted for everyone to lie face down on the floor. One jumped the bar and shouted for Margie to come to the register because he couldn't get it to open. He threatened to kill her if she didn't comply. Margie pulled the bills from each slot, including the twenties, knowing that the bill compartment was alarmed. The alarm configuration would activate when all the paper money was removed; the spring clamp that holds the bills in place would make contact with the brass plate screwed to the bottom of that part of the register drawer. When that metal-to-metal contact was made, it automatically made the necessary connection to transmit the silent signal to Ace Alarm Company's central station. Receipt of the signal indicated to the operators in the central station a robbery was in progress and they would promptly contact the police. Because the police station was only five blocks away, Margie assumed the police could arrive in no more than three minutes, if lucky.

In the meantime, the second robber was methodically searching each of the four men lying on the floor, taking watches, wallets, and searching pockets, in no particular rush.

Both Hal and Margie were worried. She knew Hal was armed. Hal knew of the silent alarm and was praying the police would arrive before the robber started to search his pockets. They both silently prayed, amid the constant flow of obscenities and insults. Hal's prayer must have been more fervent, realizing if the search revealed the gun the robber would most likely suspect he was a police officer and kill him.

The police did not arrive before the suspect came across the gun in Hal's pocket and that criminal shot Hal to death in the back of the head as he laid there on the floor. The robbers ran from the bar into the night and escaped.

The police were never informed of an alarm signal from the bar. The police weren't informed of the robbery because the alarm did not work, as designed and required. They did finally come as a result of Margie's 9-1-1 call.

Hal's family obtained an attorney who filed a civil action against the alarm company for negligently installing and/or maintaining the robbery alarm system. I was retained by that attorney and served as the security expert and expert witness. The complainant alleged, as noted earlier, negligence in the maintenance of their system.

The alarm company records, obtained through the discovery process, included a request for the production of documents that revealed the "hold-up alarm" devise installed in Benny's Place had never been tested since its installation several years earlier, despite the contract requiring inspections. Of course, the bar received a bill every month for the hold-up alarm. In my professional opinion, the failure to regularly test the alarm was negligence. Had that alarm been properly maintained it would have immediately signaled this grave event, and more likely than not, the police would have intervened and Hal's life would have been spared.

The matter settled to the benefit of the Brown family.

FUJIMOTO v. MID-PACIFIC ISLAND PRINCESS HOTEL

An attractive young tourist, Chieko Fujimoto, arrived in the idyllic paradise of the mid-Pacific and checked into an upscale hotel, the Mid-Pacific Island Princess. World War II swirled around this area in general and the island in particular. The hotel has a huge lobby open to the front to welcome incoming guests; the other side of the lobby looks out over the ocean. Palm trees are everywhere. After getting settled in Chieko decided to go shopping.

Chieko hailed a cab in the driveway in front of the hotel and asked the driver, Richie Soto, to take her to a shopping district. She sat in the front seat and, as they drove, she asked Richie where she could purchase marijuana. All the taxi drivers had been warned that "undercover spies" were being deployed to catch islanders selling dope, so he claimed ignorance of any drugs. She accepted that and spent part of the day shopping while Richie waited for her at each location. He returned her to the hotel and she spent the evening socializing with her tour group.

The Island Princess allowed taxi drivers to park and walk into the vast lobby to solicit business. Later, Chieko and the same driver spotted each other and he offered her transportation again. She again sat in the front seat. Not far from the hotel she noticed marijuana in his ashtray. Irked by his earlier claim of not having "grass," Chieko called Richie a liar. He told her to "screw off" and the verbal exchange accelerated. In a fit of anger Chieko clawed his face with both hands. Richie instantly struck back with his right hand and stopped the taxi abruptly where the two continued to battle. He choked Chieko to death and dumped her body in a remote spot on the island. He then went about his business as though nothing happened.

The next day Chieko's body was spotted and traced to the hotel. Witnesses informed the police she had been seen the day before talking to Richie in the lobby and the two disappeared together.

Richie was at home. The police asked him to come down to the police station, which he did. Richie admitted driving Chieko the first day and told the detective she asked for a ride yesterday, but he was already booked. The scratches on Richie's face aroused the detective's suspicion; when asked how they got there, Richie claimed he got scratched chasing one of his roosters.

"Brudda Richie," said the detective, "that dead lady has your skin under her fingernails. Now tell me that rooster story again and we're going to have an unpleasant relationship."

"No trouble between us, bro," replied Richie. "She was fixin' to scratch out my eyes and I had no choice but to protect myself. I choked her to make her stop scratching me. When she passed out I threw her out of the cab. I didn't mean to kill her. It was an accident."

The main cause of action in the suit brought by the victim's family was that the hotel allowed unscreened, unknown taxi drivers and strangers to enter and wander the lobby of this elegant hotel without any oversight and solicit tourists to join them for remote rides on the island. The plaintiff's theory was, had the drivers been properly screened, restricted from entering and freely mingling with the guests, and required to cue-up and await the doorman's signal when a guest needed a taxi, as is common in respectable hotels worldwide, this crime would never have happened. Bottom line, the hotel was negligent in how it controlled vendors providing services to guests.

As the expert for the attorney defending the hotel, two colleagues (investigator Skip Melberne, the premier investigator in the state of Hawaii and an expert in resort hotels, and John Takeshima, a polygraph examiner) and I departed from Honolulu with two tasks. The first was to visit the island and inspect the various luxury hotels, including, of course, the defendant property, and benchmark those hotels with Mid-Pacific Island Princess Hotel. The second task was to interview Richie in the commonwealth's penitentiary with the specific goal of getting him to again admit he committed the crime.

Richie had originally confessed and, per the presentencing agreement, was sentenced to 20 years in prison. Once Richie was named as a defendant, along with the Mid-Pacific Island Princess Hotel, in the civil action, he changed his story and claimed he was not the murderer. He retracted his confession. This retraction was a knotty issue in the defense of the hotel because it would tend to support the argument an unknown stranger from another island could have been the assailant.

With the cooperation of the warden, Melberne and I entered the prison and were guided to a table and chairs for our interview with Richie. Takeshima waited outside, standing by in the event a lie detector test was requested by Richie, something we were prepared to offer if he insisted he didn't commit the crime.

Prison officials didn't seem interested in listening, so it was a casual, open-air chat, unlike any other in-prison interviews I had experienced.

Interviews aimed at obtaining an admission when conducted by two interviewers usually evolve into a "good cop/bad cop" scenario—that is, one is more friendly and understanding than the partner. I can't recall which role I fell into, nor does it matter here. Richie at first, as expected, claimed he didn't do it. He claimed it had to do with bringing shame on his relatives, a very important issue in the culture of this island community.

We eventually brought him around to choosing which of two positions would be worst: the shame of accidentally ending someone's life, or the shame of being an intentional liar. He chose the second and admitted his retraction was not true. He did not want to be known as a liar and did not want his relatives to bear the shame of him being a liar. That task was completed.

The "benchmarking" survey of hotels on the island disclosed all the hotels' lobbies were wide open for tropical ventilation purposes. We concluded the casual island lifestyle was most permissive with respect to who could enter hotel lobbies, and the standards and practices on the U.S. mainland and other metropolitan areas simply didn't exist. As long as the taxi driver was clean, sober, and well-groomed, he or she was welcome to enter the lobby and offer excursions or rides to any interested guests. It was viewed as a service. With respect to unknown or unlicensed drivers, every resident of that island knew each other, and, it appeared, were related to each other one way or another.

The Mid-Pacific Island Princess Hotel's practices were in keeping with industry custom and practice. It was not a dangerous property, nor were any of its security measures inadequate or lacking. In my opinion the complaint lacked merit.

The matter settled to the satisfaction of all parties.

KENWORTH v. PATRIOT'S PLAZA

Patriot's Plaza is a red-brick, multi-use, four-story commercial building with a huge interior atrium in its center, from ground to ceiling. It's located in the center of what locals call Old Towne, part of a downtown renovation project. Tenants include retail shops, law offices, various cafés and small restaurants, and accounting offices, to name a few.

There's no central authority that oversees this six-square-block area of Old Towne, other than the city and its police department. The only security I saw happened to be at a bar; they were the typical door hosts who check ID and deal with intoxicated patrons or disturbances inside.

Several women visiting from out of state, including Fern Kenworth, were on a day shopping trip while their husbands attended a business conference. They found their way into Patriot's Plaza, browsed through some of the shops, made a couple little purchases, and had a light Italian lunch. Fern then asked where she might find the ladies' restroom. It was on the northeast corner of the atrium on the second floor. Stepping away from the open atrium, she went down an empty hall to the women's restroom. Further down the same hall was a men's restroom.

Fern entered the room through a single, unlockable door. Three toilet stalls were directly ahead of the entrance. The sinks were to her right, over which was hung a large mirror. Fern noted a pair of what appeared to be women's boots in the center stall. She entered an adjacent stall and, while seated on the toilet, noticed the person who had been next to her flushed the toilet and left that stall.

The next thing Fern knew the room was pitch black. The person who had been sitting in the adjacent stall had turned off the light switch. Alarmed, she yelled out, "Hey you've turned off the lights," not suspecting it was an intentional act. At that moment her stall door opened and a figure began to grope her. She struggled to pull back in the limited space, was struck in the face, and her glasses fell off. Fern screamed for help with no response. Her assailant was a man, but she couldn't see his features. For whatever reason the man released his hold, left the stall, and exited the restroom. It took a few moments for Fern to adjust her clothing and feel her way to the entrance door (she knew it was the door because the lighting outside the room illuminated the crack at the bottom). She turned on the lights, looked outside the restroom, and saw no one.

Fern returned to her friends and relayed her traumatic experience. They immediately entered a shop and asked the clerk to call the police. While waiting for the police, the group asked for the building manager and was told the property manager was in another building and not available. A police report was filed and the ladies returned to their hotel.

A lawsuit was filed against the property manager for not providing some form of security, even for some form of key control to restrict access to the restrooms, a rather common practice.

I was retained by the plaintiff's counsel, and upon my inspection of the Old Towne district in general and the Patriot's Plaza specifically, there clearly was a need for some security presence, such as a uniformed officer one would expect to find in a shopping center. Albeit minimal protection, one officer could have been a reasonable expense, and could strategically be seen moving about in the Patriot's Plaza and the six square blocks that comprised Old Towne. Two public restrooms were the only such facilities in the entire complex, and they were out of sight down a remote side hall. One flight of stairs down was an exit door from the building, so anyone could come and go without being noticed.

I inspected the interior of the men's restroom walls based on my experience as a vice officer early in my career, and found indications some sexual contacts had occurred in that room, including the presence of solicitation messages such as "Meet here Thursdays 2:30" in very small print. Infrequent inspections of the restrooms by security would have been a normal and reasonable activity. When it became known security checks of the restrooms occurred on a regular basis, sexual deviancy would go elsewhere. My opinion in this matter was there was a need for some security presence.

Had I been retained as a security management consultant to assess Old Towne and Patriot's Plaza prior to this incident, which was a major portion of my consulting practice, I would have recommended the deployment of a uniformed officer as a deterrent to crime, in keeping with custom and practice in the shopping-center industry. Of course, I was not so retained. More importantly, I was not asked a question while on the stand that would have allowed me to share what I would have done, which may have been thought-provoking for some jurors.

The plaintiff was from out of town, as was I. I could sense the local people may have been sympathetic to Fern and had no issue with my credentials or judgment, but they simply didn't want to punish the owners and management of this staid, traditional part of the city. The defense attorney argued this was a totally unforeseeable incident and there was no duty to provide security. This is a common defense position, depending on the circumstances of course, and indeed that has been my position in some cases.

The jury found for the Patriot's Plaza.

HERNANDEZ v. JUNE DEPARTMENT STORES

The armored car arrived in the service alley at 11:45 a.m., its scheduled time to pick up the daily deposit for June Department Store, prepared by the cashiers in the secured cash office. The store was located on the corner of a major intersection. The front of the store had two sets of double doors and faced north on a major boulevard. The west side of the store had two sets of double doors and faced a highly trafficked boulevard. The east side had one set of doors; it bordered an active alley and service corridor.

The three-story store opened at 9:00 a.m. and two plainclothes store detectives, equipped with two-way radios, inconspicuously patrolled the store's three floors and basement. Both were on duty when the armored truck arrived, even though they weren't aware of the truck's arrival, nor should they have been. Their focus was on customers browsing the store, looking for indications of possible shoplifting.

The driver, Billy Brown, remained in the truck with the engine running while the second guard, Carlos Hernandez, dressed in his uniform and cap, exited the vehicle through the cargo compartment door located on the passenger's side. Once he closed that door it self-locked, requiring a key to reenter the truck with the "coal bag" containing the store's bank deposit bags.

Carlos was an experienced armored car guard and had been properly trained. He carried the empty canvas bag in his left hand while his right hand rested on the handle of his .38 caliber revolver. He entered the store through the single set of eastern doors, turned left, and walked south past the cashier's window to the cashier office door with a small 10×10 inch window and pushed the button. The head cashier, Mary Fiorini, looked through the interior door window and, recognizing the guard, buzzed open the first door.

Carlos was now in a "man-trap" (a short hallway between two locked doors), and, in keeping with policy, he now exhibited his armored service company credentials. Mary, in the cashiering vault area, released the latch and allowed him access. Carlos set about his duties of signing for the numbered sealed bags and placed them in his "coal bag." The canvas bag is similar in size and construction to a firewood bag one finds in homes with fireplaces. It should be noted at some stops a dolly is required to wheel the bags because of the weight, especially in businesses that frequently use coins. The bank bags on this trip, as usual and as expected, were not heavy, but they did contain currency and bank checks amounting to thousands of dollars.

At about 11:00 a.m., prior to the truck's arrival, two men entered the store through separate doors and browsed the displayed merchandise on that main floor. Neither of the two were unusual in appearance nor were they acting suspicious. In the normal course of events both men came under brief surveillance by each of the two store security agents, but there was no indication in their behavior they might be shoplifters or considering shoplifting. Rather, they appeared to be "killing time" waiting for someone. This store, located in a major metropolitan area, had heavy foot traffic. It was often a meeting place because of its reputation, location, and a lunch room on the third floor.

Carlos, now with the bag in his left hand and his right hand on his gun handle, was buzzed out the cashier's room inner door, then again buzzed through the door leading onto the sales floor. As he commenced the long walk northbound back to the set of doors facing out to the waiting armored truck, the two male customers approached Carlos from his rear left side, each carrying a handgun. Before he realized what was occurring, they shot him dead inside the store, snatched the "coal bag," ran across the store to the doors on the west side, and disappeared.

Because the walkie-talkie radios were both "open," Billy thought he heard shots but wasn't sure exactly what had happened. He called Carlos, but there was no response. Billy immediately called his office, who called the police.

The Hernandez family filed a lawsuit against the store alleging negligence for (1) scheduling an armored car to arrive at a predictable time each day, therefore facilitating the likelihood of a planned robbery; (2) the two security agents were negligent by allowing single strangers to wander aimlessly for nearly an hour without making a purchase; (3) trained security officers should have realized an armored car was due, because of its regularly scheduled visit, and should have called the police before the incident as a preventative measure; and (4) the store's agents should have been armed and, had they been armed, they could have shot the robbers either before the hold-up or as they fled through the store.

I was retained as the store's expert witness. A university professor teaching criminal justice was the plaintiff's expert.

The professor testified in deposition that the agents should have been armed, should have realized the two men could be waiting for the armored car, and could (and should) have prevented this tragedy if they had been properly trained. He also testified that store detectives should escort armored guards to and from the cashiering operation and, had they done so, while armed, the robbery and death would not have happened. The professor admitted he had no private sector experience or retail experience.

I testified in deposition that store detectives were never armed and the local police would object to such employees carrying guns; indeed, the state law prohibited the use of guns by these private citizens. I testified that the protection of daily receipts and bank deposits was outside the area of responsibility of store detectives; indeed, that's why specialists in securing and transporting money were contracted out to the armored car company. I testified security agents are trained for the classic indicators of possible shoplifting and their failure to suspect the two "customers" of being armed robbers was fully understandable, especially in view of the fact store detectives had no information about, interest in, or duty to be aware of armored truck schedules or even the risk of such an event. Considering it was the first robbery and death of an armored truck guard in this chain store's history, I also testified it was an extraordinary event.

The attorney representing the store was so persuaded by my testimony that his case was a "slam-dunk" defense, he didn't bother to call me to testify during the trial.

According to the report and discussions post-trial, the decision to go "bare," i.e. not produce an expert, was a fatal trial error. The jury was most impressed with a criminal justice professor, and his testimony and opinions went unchallenged. The jury found the store negligent in not arming their security personnel and not training them to help protect the daily bank deposit. To this day, I roll my eyes when I think of that professor's opinions and the jury's decision.

The store was held liable for the death of the guard.

BROWN v. ELANTA DEPARTMENT STORES

Elanta Department Stores, a fashion department store chain, followed the unusual protection strategy of using off-duty police officers to patrol the interior of their stores, as opposed to the more traditional strategy of deploying in-house store detectives and investigators. The upside of using officers for the company was avoiding costs of normal employee benefits, such as vacation and sick pay, health insurance, and a retirement program. They also had the unusual benefit of having local police service in store and under their control. Additionally, it was more likely the store would enjoy some immunity against a lawsuit in the event an officer stopped a customer for shoplifting when the customer in fact had not stolen any merchandise.

The downside of using police officers was their demand for a much higher hourly wage than a regular employee because they viewed their time on the job in the store as "time and a half." Put another way, they were expensive. Another negative factor was an officer scheduled for a given shift at times couldn't show up for work because of the demands of the police department, such as an emergency or unexpected event. Then the store had to go without security or scramble to find a last-minute substitute. Working for the store was a far lower priority than that of the officer's primary employer—the city police department or county sheriff's department.

Because the ongoing cost of two police officers in each store during store hours was considerable, the company's finance division developed a new strategy of using TV cameras operated by regular civilian employees and deploying only one police officer at a time. The company purchased and installed the cameras and published a job description that mandated the camera operator could not leave the camera room. If the operator observed someone conceal or attempt to steal merchandise, that information would be forwarded to the police officer in the store, who would deal with the culprit. On the face of it the plan seemed reasonable, but in reality there were frequent occasions when what the camera operator saw and reported was not a theft, and the customer stopped by the police was most indignant, to say the least. However, the police officer, because of his or her authority, could smooth over the mistake, something a store's loss prevention agent couldn't do.

Invariably, there were times when the police officer scheduled to work simply didn't show up for work and only the store camera operator was on duty. Store management didn't want to engage in security work, so they ignored the job description and instructed the operator to go ahead and leave his or her post and go onto the selling floor to make detentions. Some managers went so far as to purchase metal policelike badges that read "Elanta Police" for the camera operators.

One newly hired part-time camera operator, Jason Peters, a local city fireman, regularly worked alone without a police officer in the store. Jason made a number of detentions for shoplifting and was praised by the store manager for his work, although company policy prohibited camera operators from making detentions.

Early one evening, Jason was working alone. He observed an attractive young woman, later identified as Janelle Brown, place an item of merchandise, a red wallet, in her coat pocket. Jason left the camera room, located Janelle on the selling floor, displayed his Atlanta police badge, and escorted her up to the privacy of the camera room located on the second floor of the store. Janelle surrendered the stolen wallet when he asked for it. Company policy specifically stated no female should be questioned or processed without the presence of another woman to serve as a witness. This policy was designed to ensure against any subsequent claims of indecent suggestions, remarks, or other impropriety. Jason was aware of the policy.

Jason completed the required paperwork for a person in custody. When done, instead of calling the police to report what had happened, Jason put down the pen and informed the worried and upset detainee, in very descriptive and obscene language, that if she would not submit to sexual intercourse he would call the police, and they would take her to jail. Literally terrified and crying, Janelle stated she would rather go to jail.

Jason arose from his desk chair and instructed Janelle to accompany him. They left the camera room and climbed the stairs to the fourth floor. She quietly wept and her body shook as they went up the stairs. There were no employees in the area. This floor wasn't open to the public, but, rather, was used for some stock and storage, dimly lit, and was rarely visited by employees.

In a remote part of that floor was the storage area for the display department's various props, including seasonal decorations like a sled and reindeer. Near those displays Jason forced Janelle to undress, by intimidation and threats of bodily harm, and raped her on folded furniture mats lying on the floor. She was crying throughout the ordeal.

When done, Jason allowed her to dress. He returned Janelle to the security camera room, reminded her he knew her address from the detention report, and threatened her and her family if she told anyone what had transpired. Jason said he would tear up the report for the police and she was free to leave the store. He escorted Janelle to the front door and saw her off.

Janelle walked to the corner and down the side street and west side of the large store and reentered. She approached an employee behind a counter in the jewelry department and said she had been raped and needed to see the store manager. The manager appeared, and when he saw how upset Janelle was and when she said she had been raped by the security officer, he immediately took her to his office and called the police.

By the time the police arrived, Jason had completed his shift and left the store.

Detectives found the detention report identifying Janelle and noted that Jason had logged the arrest on a clipboard bearing the names of all persons arrested month-to-date. Jason was subsequently arrested, charged with rape, prosecuted, changed his plea to guilty at the time of trial, and was sentenced to 15 years in the state penitentiary.

Janelle retained legal counsel, who commenced a search for a retail security expert. I agreed to being retained. The task for the expert was to assess the protection program to determine if the store was in any way exposed to liability or responsible for the conduct of its employees. Was the store negligent? More often than not, a plaintiff law firm will draw up a complaint and causes of action without the benefit of an expert's input and subsequently locate and retain the expert. The expert, when queried, will either agree or disagree with the theory of liability and, in that discussion, the attorney may decide to retain or not retain the expert. Both sides make a choice.

Once a lawsuit is filed, counsel for the defendant will commence his or her search for the same kind of expert, and the battle lines are drawn and the process of discovery commences. The end result of the process of discovery is the expert forms his or her opinions and each side is provided with those opinions. An expert's opinions can, in and of themselves, persuade one side or the other to avoid trial and settle.

My numerous findings and subsequent opinions in this matter included, but were not limited, to:

- The security program lacked professional guidance and leadership—that is, there was no trained professional security executive at the corporate level to oversee the program, including its budget, policies, procedures, personnel, and training.
- Absent leadership and typical organizational design, there was no way to verify or oversee store-level performance by those hired to work in the stores.
- Absent levels of organizational security supervision, there was no way to ensure compliance with procedures and policy. As an example, any regional supervisor would have discovered, by simple examination of security records, arrests were being made by unauthorized personnel. Any regional or district supervisor, in reviewing arrest/detention paperwork generated at the store level, would quickly discover that not only were unauthorized employees stopping and detaining customers, but policies such as a female witness being required when a woman is in custody were being ignored.

The bottom line: the store's security/loss prevention program was below the industry's standard of care and failure to oversee and supervise security staff amounted to gross negligence. The matter settled.

WASHINGTON v. CRESTVIEW COUNTRY CLUB

Hank and Millie Washington and their two daughters, 19-year-old Kenesha and 22-year-old Cherese, resided in the exclusive and private community of Crestview Country Club. They were one of four African-American families who were property owners in that community. The heads of these households were professionals, and they all were active in the social activities of Crestview. Hank and Millie both had Ph.D. degrees from prestigious universities, and Millie was a popular partner in the women's golf club with her nine handicap.

There were three entrances through which all traffic entered and exited the property. The main entrance, the west gate, was used primarily by residents and their guests; the east gate was used primarily by vendors, employees, and a wide range of service vehicles, such as lawn maintenance, pool maintenance, plumbers, electricians, etc.; and the north gate was remote, at the backside of the country club, and was sparsely used by any vehicle bearing the required windshield decal or individual whose name or company was on the daily gate entry list.

Each gate was staffed and controlled by security. The main gatehouse at the west gate was typically staffed by three officers, the east gate gatehouse was staffed by two officers, and the north gate had a small gatehouse room for only a single officer who could sit on a stool during the long periods of time between a vehicle entering or leaving. They were all well-lit during hours of darkness.

When a vehicle approached the main gate, drivers would be directed to the entry road next to the gatehouse and the officer would step out of the gatehouse; and if the vehicle displayed a residential decal, it was waved through without the need to stop. If no decal was on the windshield, the officer would inquire as to why—for example, if the auto was a loaner or belonged to some family member who did not live in the community. In those cases, a temporary sign was placed on the dashboard and the car would proceed in. If the vehicle was driven by a guest it would enter the designated guest lane and the officer would approach the driver, determine his or her business, compare the driver to the daily gate entry list, issue a temporary one-day permit, and the vehicle was allowed into the property. When the visitor exited the property there was no requirement or need for the temporary permit to be returned because it was dated.

A similar entrance procedure was in place at the east and north gates, although there was only one lane to enter and a different colored decal or pass was required for nonresidents.

The issue of authorized access was important to the homeowners' association. Monthly meetings, as well as the weekly community newsletter, invariably addressed the responsibility of residents to arrange for passage if they were going to change vehicles and remember to advise the main gate of anticipated visitors so they could be logged. Residents were reminded of the need to comply with the association's rules and officers' directions. On those exceptional incidents when an unauthorized vehicle slipped through or was allowed in, that was highlighted in the newsletter. Some people joked at the notion that even the governor couldn't enter unless he had a decal or his name was on the list.

The Washingtons were long-time residents of Crestview; their daughters grew up there. When Kenesha was a freshman in college she met a young man at a party, James Cooper, who was not a college student. Kenesha brought him home to meet her parents. Mr. and Mrs. Washington were concerned that James wasn't "going anywhere." Although it was awkward for them, she would invite him over, arrange for him to obtain a vehicle pass, and visit with the family. James was Kenesha's first serious boyfriend, and she was in love. Kenesha tried to tactfully warn her about getting too attached and to encourage her see and date other young men, but to no avail. It wasn't long before their worst fears were realized. Kenesha became pregnant and, for reasons never clear to the family, James ended up in jail. As best they could tell, it had to do with narcotics.

Before and after the birth of her baby, Kenesha kept in contact with James by writing to him and they had occasional phone conversations, but the relationship cooled when he started persisting she drop out of college and marry him when he was released. He was also asking for money.

Unexpectedly, James was released and told Kenesha he wanted to see the baby. She arranged for him to enter the country club. James arrived in a somewhat pricey collector's car, a yellow English MG roadster. Their first meeting after his release from jail was cordial, but stiff. James made over the baby, while the family awkwardly sat around the living room engaged in small talk. James and Kenesha stepped outside for a short time and started to argue in hushed tones about her quitting school and his insistence on living together. James was demanding, rude, and on the verge of being threatening. Everyone was relieved when he left, but he promised to return.

After a couple more visits so James could see the baby, Kenesha broke off their relationship. James became abusive on the phone and said he was entitled to see his son and he would come over, no matter what she said. In that argument Kenesha reminded him he had failed to provide any support for his child and, until he did, he wouldn't see his son again. James was so angry and loud that Kenesha was trembling when the conversation ended and, for the first time, she felt uneasy over her and the baby's safety.

Because of his threat to visit, invited or not, Kenesha informed her family, who decided to prepare a notice for the security department to deny access to the property at the entrance gates. Kenesha had a colored photo of James standing next to the yellow MG. Millie crafted a warning notice with the photo, name, and description of James, stating he should not be allowed access to the club property. It further stated if James appeared at any gate, the officer should phone the Washingtons. Their phone number was prominently displayed. The notice was signed on the bottom by Millie and dated.

Kenesha and Cherese met with the captain of the security force and informed him they were afraid James would come to their home and could be violent. The posting of similar notices wasn't unusual, but neither was it common. They asked if he would post the warnings in the gate-houses. The captain said he would and the sisters returned home with a sense of relief.

Ten days later, two Sundays before Christmas, Hank arose early in the morning, made coffee, read part of the Sunday morning paper, and went to pick up the Christmas tree the family had selected the day before. His wife and daughters slept in.

About one hour after leaving, Hank returned home with the tree tied to the top of the car. As he turned the corner on which his house stood, he noticed the front door appeared partially open, which struck him as peculiar. Instead of entering the garage (because of the tree on his car's roof) he parked in the driveway and walked to the front door. To his utter shock his wife, wearing her nightgown and robe, was lying immediately inside the door in a pool of blood. It was apparent she had a massive wound to her face from a gunshot. Barely alive, she moved ever so slightly. In a state of panic, Hank ran down the hall to the closest phone and called 9-1-1, shouting for medical assistance. He then ran to the hallway that led to his daughters' rooms and discovered Cherese lying partially in the bed-room and partially in the hall, as though she had come to the door to see what the noise was about. She was in her nightgown, covered with blood, dead. Like in a nightmare, he ran to Kenesha's room. She was par-tially covered with the sheet and blankets, but she too had been shot and was motionless. The baby was untouched.

Emergency, rescue, and police personnel were soon on the horrific scene. Millie survived, but with facial scaring, some speech impediment, and nightmares.

The first and immediate question was: Who would do such a thing?

Hank provided all the information he had on James. Two days later James was arrested and booked for suspicion of homicide.

A law firm known to the Washingtons was contacted and within a year a complaint was filed against James, the Crestview Country Club homeowners' association, and Fidelity Security Company, the contractor that provided security services on the property.

The complaint against James, for damages, was a given. The thrust of the complaint against the other two defendants was for negligence—that is, failure to provide adequate security as required by allowing James to enter the property and commit the crime. Had they restricted his access and denied him entry, the crime, more likely than not, wouldn't have occurred.

I was retained by the plaintiffs (the Washingtons) as a security consultant and possible expert witness, assuming my investigation convinced me the theory of security negligence was meritorious.

My task was to review every document generated in the discovery process, which included the police murder book (the collection of every police report, photos, maps, measurements, etc.). Documents also include reports of all interviews, all depositions taken of witnesses, all records and reports maintained by the security department, the homeowners' association's minutes of their meetings ... ad infinitum. I also visited the property to inspect the guardhouses, patrol procedures, bulletin boards, post orders, and historical records of incidents and issued permanent parking permits as well as visitor parking passes.

My review of police reports revealed that during their early investigation, the rather confused and distraught Hank, the only witness who was able to provide any information, including his suspicion of James, recalled Millie had told him about giving security a warning poster to keep James from coming in. The warning posted in the main gatehouse was taken as evidence. There was no mention of the other two gatehouses.

Among the records was clear evidence that James was the assailant, despite his denial, and he was speedily convicted and sentenced to life imprisonment for the murder of his child's mother, her sister, and the felonious assault with a firearm against Millie. James was never deposed because, not long after he was interviewed by the homeowners' association's lawyer, James was murdered in prison. Whatever he shared about the event with counsel was forever protected as lawful, privileged communication between client and attorney. That was a blow to the plaintiff's case because, if he was truthful, valuable evidence could be introduced about how he entered the property.

The essence of the defendant's position was there was no negligence, there was no proof or evidence the assailant entered through any secured gate, and, if James was the assailant, he had to scale a perimeter fence to get to the Washington's home. The perimeter fence, a wire-topped cyclone fence, was a reasonable and universally accepted barrier to deter intruders. Warning notices to deny access were honored in the normal course of their gate control procedures. The club's security procedures and practices were in keeping with or above the security standards of care in environments similar to this private country club and residential area. The bottom line: they were not negligent.

After all my work, I concluded, based on the report of an almost insignificant police interview with the guard, Lyle Oosten, that James entered through the north gate. Oosten was on duty at the remote north gate in the early-morning hours of the crime; a detective conducted that interview two days after the shooting.

After some preliminary comments about the importance of the investigation, the detective asked a very nervous Oosten if many cars came through his gate during those early-morning hours. Oosten said he had a few come through. He was asked if a yellow MG roadster driven by a young black man had come through his gate, and said he didn't remember. Oosten, an elderly gentleman, was assigned to this particular post because it was less demanding than the much busier gates, and he wasn't capable of patrolling the community in a radio car.

In my view, Oosten wasn't telling the detective the truth about the yellow car because he feared for his job and was afraid to be held in any way responsible for the deaths of the girls. His answer of "I don't remember" regarding the question about that very distinctive, unusual car driven by a young black man (particularly considering) there were very few black residents in that community) during the typically quiet early-morning hours was not plausible. If indeed no such car came through his gate, the answer should have been, "No such car came through my gate while I was on duty. You might want to check with Harry Smith who gave me a 30-minute lunch break. Maybe it came through then." During my deposition, under oath, I was pressed by the defense attorney as to how I could say the car was allowed to slip through a secured gate without absolute proof. My response was it was a matter of judgment. It was based on the preponderance of information that James was the assailant. He had to drive about 40 miles to get to the property, and it was most unlikely he would or could scale the fence and leave his car exposed along a fence line. It would be a difficult chore to walk the two miles from the closest fence line, in the dark, commit the crime, and then repeat the hike. It was my opinion he couldn't get in the main gate but knew about the alternate entrance. I opined that he drove to the north gate. The security guard would have seen the headlight approaching and come out of his shack. The driver could have displayed an earlier temporary pass through the window, and the older gentleman waved him through. Or, he stopped and the older gentleman came out and they visited (it's lonely out there), and then was convinced by the fast-talking James it was okay for him to enter. I recall so clearly how this defense attorney and I looked at each other, eye to eye, for what seemed like a long time, and then she went on with other questions. She volunteered that her security expert said he had no way of knowing if the assailant entered via a gate and he went so far as to say, "Who knows, the murderer could have even parachuted in," and laughed.

The matter never went to trial. It settled.

Postscript: A year or two later I had occasion to talk with the attorney who had originally retained me on this case. He informed me the defense attorney who stared at me when I offered my opinion had talked with James in prison as his defense attorney in this civil case. This was just before James was killed. James had told her he approached the north gate, the old gentleman came out, James commented on how cold and lonely he must be out there, they had a congenial visit, James showed him his old temporary pass, said he was a regular visitor, and the guard let him in. She *knew* as our eyes were fixed on each other, my opinion was dead on. Surely, as we looked at each other she had to consider my opinion uncanny, and how could I possibly know?

CHAPTER 12

A Summarization of Cases Based on Inadequate Security and/or Breach of Duty as the Theory of Liability

Contents

MULLINS v. CITY LIBRARY

The plaintiff and her nine-year-old daughter went to the city library, a regular event each week. On the day in question she noted her daughter had been missing for some time. She walked the facility and, not seeing her daughter, she reported her concern to the head librarian. Security for the library was a woman whose task was to patrol the two floors and ensure order, mostly with youngsters using the facility. This security woman was asked to search the entire library for the missing girl. She did, but came up empty-handed. The mother then asked if she had checked the men's restroom downstairs.

"No," replied the woman.

"Why not?"

"I can't go into the men's room."

A quick search of that room found the child lying in an enclosed commode, crying. She had been raped on the floor by a teenage boy.

Following that incident the parents filed a civil complaint against the library claiming it lacked adequate security and crimes on premises were foreseeable. That very restroom had a history of vandalism over the preceding month, including a recent incident where feces and been spread on the walls, mirrors, and wash fixtures. Toilets had also been intentionally plugged and obscenities written on the walls. No similar problems occurred in the women's restroom.

Among other crimes that required the police to respond was the incident when a man was detected crawling on the floor under the reading tables, looking up women's dresses.

I prepared my report, pointing out that men's restrooms are known for perverse sexual contacts and conduct, in any environment such as public parks, movie theaters, department stores, and city halls, based on my years as a vice officer in Los Angeles, CA. In my opinion, the youthful clientele of this library was aware the female security officer did not check the men's room, which made it a safe haven for mischief. A properly trained female security officer would be cognizant of the risks and indeed find a way to include that room in her rounds, such as propping the door open, announcing intent to enter, and, if necessary, obtaining the assistance of the maintenance staff to accompany her. To not regularly check the room was negligence. I opined that some form of assault in that room was foreseeable.

Counsel for the city library filed a motion for dismissal of the complaint on the grounds this unusual and one-of-a-kind assault was simply not foreseeable and therefore there was no breach of duty.

The matter was dismissed.

JAMES v. SILVER DISCOUNT STORES

It was early evening Christmas Eve. Elva James needed to purchase a star or angel for the very top of her Christmas tree, the final touch for her Christmas decorations. She parked in the lot directly in front of a Silver Discount store and had to walk a short distance to reach the sidewalk and front doors. Considering it was Christmas Eve, there weren't that many last-minute shoppers. She made her purchase and didn't notice anyone in the area as she walked back to her car. As she stood next to the driver's door, she bent her head down and searched her purse for her keys. Once she located the key ring she opened the door and started to get in when "out of nowhere" a man appeared from behind, pushing her in and following close behind. He forced her over the front seat divider and gear shift lever while maintaining a firm grasp of her coat so she couldn't continue out the passenger side. In this action, he threatened her life if she screamed. He demanded the keys and drove out of the lot with her cowering next to him. She begged him not to hurt her, to please let her go, that he could keep the car, and that her family was waiting at home for her. With a raised voice he told her if she wanted to see her family again, all she had to do was keep quiet and cooperate. She detected alcohol on his breath as he shouted at her.

He turned into a residential area not far from the store where he stopped and three more men entered the car. They were loud and appeared to be intoxicated, laughing and talking about how they just got out of Santa's sleigh, saying "Ho, Ho, Ho," and what fun they were having tonight.

She was driven to a remote rural area on the outskirts of town where the driver pulled the car under a large tree. The men stripped her naked and she was gang-raped on the ground.

Following the assault they drove off in her car, leaving her alone in the dark without her clothing. Traumatized and desperate, she stumbled across a large plowed field, ran toward a house with lighted windows, and screamed for help. The residents came out, took her in, and called the police.

She was taken to the emergency room of the nearest hospital for a rape kit, and was clinically medicated and sedated. The hospital contacted her husband, who picked her up after arranging for a relative to come over and stay with their children, because "Mom had been in an accident." At the suggestion of the police, a locksmith was called to rekey the house.

The next morning the police located her car, but her clothes, purse, the bag with the ornament, and her key ring, which included a key to her house, were never found. The assailants were never identified or located. The plaintiff filed a lawsuit charging that this free-standing big-box store had a duty to provide security for its patrons inside as well as outside the store.

The store countered it had a professional loss prevention/security staff, they were on duty at the very time of the abduction, and therefore, were not remiss or negligent. Indeed, for the Christmas season they hired a local off-duty police officer whose very duties included checking the cars in the parking lot.

My research into the history of police service calls for that store and other businesses up and down the boulevard for one mile in each direction from the defendant store revealed an extraordinary number of crimes in the parking areas in that store lot, specifically, and in the parking areas of neighboring businesses, generally.

Further research disclosed the chief of police of the city in which this store was located had his own "moonlight" guard service, on the side, and had approached the store suggesting they consider using his service to protect the parking lot. The chief actually told the regional loss prevention manager the store was in a high-crime area. They opted not to use the chief's private security service because they were of the opinion the service was a conflict of interest and was unethical.

I testified the store's position that the chief's offer was questionable was understandable, but once advised the area had a growing crime problem, the store should have been prompted to conduct their own crime-rate investigation, and if the chief's assertion was true, they should have taken extra protective measures to protect both employees and patrons in the lot.

I also testified the entire protection effort was devoted to theft detection inside the store and, despite being warned by the police, no outside security was provided. I also went on record with my opinion that parking lots are inherently prone to crime victimization, especially during the holiday seasons. I pointed out the only checking of the lot by the police officer was when he took his cigarette breaks and stood with his back against the building looking out toward the parked cars, meaning he never went out into the lot and was never seen in the lot, therefore there was no crime deterrent value while he smoked on the sidewalk. In my opinion, the lot was not properly protected.

The matter settled favorably for the plaintiff.

HOLLOMAN v. AMERICAN GAS STATIONS

The plaintiff is an elderly woman who lived in a mobile-home park with her daughter. Early one morning she told her daughter she was out of cigarettes and was going to walk over to the gas station and purchase a pack. Her daughter told her it was still dark outside, so she couldn't go. The older woman slipped away while her daughter was preoccupied, walked to a major intersection, and crossed the street to the gas station. In front of the building on one corner she noted a man slumped on the bus bench. It was barely dawn. As she passed behind him he got up from the bench and jumped on her back, forcing her to fall on the macadam surface of the gas station. While in that hunched-over position, with the woman pinned underneath him, he pulled both of her eyes from their sockets.

The driver of an 18-wheeler saw the man jump on the woman and brought his big rig to a bouncing stop, grabbed the rubber hammer he used to test his tires, and pursued the assailant. He saw the assailant run into a fast-food restaurant and caught him in the men's restroom washing blood from his hands.

The gas station was open for business, but the attendant was tilted back in a wooden chair, asleep, and missed the event. The family sued the station for inadequate security.

The plaintiff's security expert did a statistical crime analysis of all known crimes reported to the police in that specific jurisdiction and compared them to the surrounding jurisdictions. This particular district, a mostly commercial area, ranked in the upper 20th percentile—that is, a relatively high risk for crime.

He pointed out the station had no CCTV cameras or alarm systems and never deployed a guard on their property, all of which would have been reasonable in view of the area in which it was located, and therefore the level of security was insufficient and inadequate.

I acknowledged the area was prone to crime, but for a gas station that only sold gasoline, batteries, and other small sundry items, located on a large busy corner, it did not need a guard, cameras, or central station alarm equipment. Such a security strategy was both economically unfeasible and unreasonable. No other gas station in the city had such security.

The plaintiff's security expert was particularly critical of the station employee who was seated inside the station facing the incident, allegedly asleep. He suggested the man wasn't sleeping, but rather was afraid to intervene. I privately agreed with that notion. This employee seemed shifty.

I personally interviewed the owner of the station who had an excellent command of the English language and was bright. However, when he appeared in court to testify he requested an interpreter because English was not his first language, and every question to him, as well as his responses to those questions, had to be interpreted. He appeared evasive and, again, shifty. To this day I'm convinced the jury did not like or trust him or his brother-in-law, the station attendant.

The jury found for the plaintiff.

JONES v. HIGHLIGHT CASINO AND HOTEL

Friday nights were "family pizza night" in Dominic's, one of the restaurants in the Highlight Casino and Hotel complex. The weekly plan for the Jones family was to enjoy a pizza dinner at the casino. The Jones family included three children: 11-year-old Tommy, 10-year-old Greta, and 7-year-old Teri.

Following dinner, the parents would go into the casino proper, where children are not allowed, and the kids would go to the children's amusement arcade, each with $10 to play the various games of their individual choice. Each of the kids had their favorite machines. Invariably, they split up. Tommy was supposed to "keep an eye" on his sisters. Between games, he would periodically wander the building to see that they were okay.

The arcade was in a separate building situated between the casino and the two-story hotel complex. The entrance to the arcade was approximately 150 feet from the casino's side door leading to Dominic's. There was a second arcade door, mainly used as an exit, which led toward the swimming pool surrounded by a lawn in the center of the hotel. Casino guests parked their cars around the arcade and across the street in the parking ramp. Hotel guests parked their cars around the exterior of the horseshoe-shaped hotel building.

The arcade's interior layout was unusual in that it was like a large house with various rooms, as opposed to being one large hall. Tommy, when he did his infrequent checks on his sisters, had to weave in and out of various rooms.

About an hour and a half after the children entered the arcade, well after sunset, Tommy found Teri near the entrance door, disheveled and quietly crying. He noticed the back of her dress was dirty, with some leaves clinging to the material. She had a crumbled-up $5 bill in her hand. He asked her what was wrong and how she got so dirty. She said a "nasty" man had taken her outside, made her lay down on the ground, and got on top of her.

Tommy took her arm and led her through the casino side door, past Dominic's, to the gaming floor where he saw a uniformed security officer, and told him his sister had been hurt by a man and asked the guard to page his parents.

The parents were horrified when they saw their daughter and obtained her story. Teri said she ran out of money and, while she was looking at a machine, a man came along and asked her why she wasn't playing. She told him she had no more money. He put in a coin so she could play a game, and then said he needed help to unload some groceries from the trunk of his car to take up to his hotel room. He offered her $5 to help him. Teri jumped at the chance to get the extra money so she could continue playing and agreed.

She followed him out of the arcade through the rear exit, across part of the lawn to the west wing of the hotel, and to the single row of parked cars facing the hotel. Midway down the line of cars he took her arm and pulled her across the narrow driveway to the complex property line designated by a long row of trees. By now it was dark outside and there were no lights along the tree line. Teri became alarmed and tried to pull away. When she started to cry the man said, "I know your family and I'll kill them if you don't do as I say. You want them to die?" He put her on the ground, got down on his knees, put his hand inside her underwear, and then climbed on top of her. She told her mother he "bounced on her." The police were contacted and one of the responding officers was a female detective. Teri was so emotionally stunned that every bit of information had to be coaxed from her by the detective and her mother. She was so traumatized she didn't want to talk.

Teri was immediately taken to the hospital where it was determined there had been no sexual penetration, but semen was collected from her clothing. She was sedated and the family went home.

A lawsuit was promptly filed against the Highlight Casino and Hotel for failure to provide an adequate level of security to protect children in an environment established just for them, knowing full well child molesters and pedophiles were known to haunt such places. I was retained to represent the child and her parents.

Examination of the security officer schedules revealed no officer was assigned to the arcade. Numerous officers were assigned to various sections of the casino, parking ramp, hotel complex, and casino cashiering operation, but the arcade was not included in the protection program, except for the deployment of cameras, which did indeed provide full coverage of that operation. The camera system was not manned, but rather memorialized all activity for postevent review, or the system could be manned live if an event was suspected.

A review of all the videotapes for the period of time confirmed the girl's story of being approached by a man and engaging in conversation with him. By patching together the videotapes from several cameras, one could see the child following the man through the arcade and out the exit. Twenty-three minutes later she was seen reentering the arcade and standing near the doors.

The casino contended the arcade employees were charged with overseeing the children and there was no indication the assailant was engaged in any suspicious behavior. However, my review of the videotapes revealed the culprit walked through the arcade several times, often stopping to watch the girls, then continue out, only to reenter after a lapse of 15–25 minutes. Clearly, his focus was on young girls, but the two arcade employees were occupied with the business of making change and keeping the games functional to notice.

Videotapes also confirmed that no security officer was in the building except when escorting money from the main casino to the cashier's back office that happened to be in the arcade building. That office was a secured cash-counting room and no security officer was assigned there. Once the funds were taken into that room the security officer would exit the arcade, returning to his or her assignment back inside the main casino.

In my mind, all such findings established the fact the arcade failed to provide adequate security for children who were "parked there" while their parents gambled. I was also critical of the training of security officers in general and the arcade employees specifically, as mandated by a new county code. This code, enacted after the sexual assault and murder of a girl in a hotel–casino operation in another part of the state, required the chief of security to hold child molestation awareness sessions and document that training in terms of the date, time, and trainer in each employee's personnel file. Examination of the personnel files disclosed only a handful of officers were so "trained" by the chief himself, and then, for some unknown reason, the training program stopped.

Whereas I was critical of the security department's failure to provide adequate security for the arcade, I did credit them with their investigative success in identifying the assailant. The video image of the man leading Teri out of the arcade was the same man on another video where he was standing at the register with his wife while paying for their meal with a credit card. That transaction revealed the man's name. A guest was registered in the hotel with the same name. The police were advised, and they determined the man was on parole for a similar offense. The man was arrested and admitted his involvement with the child.

Following my sworn testimony in deposition, the matter settled.

FRANCHETTI v. SUNSET HOTEL CASINO

Virginia Higgins and her boyfriend, Ricky Christman, had originally been attracted to the glitzy lights and excitement of the big hotel casinos. Being on a limited budget, they took up residency in a cheap motel. Virginia was unsuccessful in her attempts to get a job in one the big hotels' chorus lines, despite her attractiveness. She had to settle for a job as a cocktail waitress. Ricky was lazy, almost too lazy to shoplift, but he did provide some income from peddling his stolen merchandise. The two regularly used cocaine, and the cost of that habit severely restricted the lifestyle they felt they were entitled to in a city in which everyone seemed to have an abundance of money.

Virginia could make good tips but couldn't hold down a job because she was unreliable. Each day of unemployment, coupled with the ever-demanding need for drugs, seemed like a neverending downward spiral. Their financially cramped life went from bad to worse when Ricky's long-time friend Gary Graham was released on parole and moved in with them. The three shared one car, but they couldn't afford the insurance.

While the three lounged in the motel room, filled with cigarette smoke, Gary had an idea. What if Virginia could entice high-rollers to leave the casino with the understood expectation of having sex? It seemed like a reasonable plan to have her entice well-heeled, well-groomed gentlemen to join her in her "apartment" for an evening of fun. Her task was to lead the "trick" to their car parked in a dark section of the parking lot, where her two accomplices would be waiting. Once out in the parking lot, Ricky and Gary would "roll" the man, relieving him of his wallet and jewelry. Ricky had a gun, but it was agreed no one would get hurt; the gun would be used to scare the victim and get his immediate compliance and cooperation. This was a variation of the old-fashioned "paddy hustle," in which the victim's clothing would be quietly searched and valuables removed by an accomplice during the act of intercourse. In this plan, no sex was going to occur. This would be an out-and-out simple robbery.

Now, solicitation in casino environments wasn't a novel or original scheme. The beauty of their plan was Virginia didn't look or dress like a classic hooker and the vice cops didn't know her because she had no record in town. She had to be cautious not to hit on a vice officer, but that wasn't a problem because the target for their operation would always be a well-dressed man, typically with expensive clothing, shoes, and jewelry. Vice cops could dress nicely, but not to the level of the model they had in mind. Indeed, it seemed the plan was flawless. Why not try it that night?

Virginia changed from her sweats into her nicest outfit and the three drove to the Sunset Hotel Casino, a huge complex, where they found the darkest lot on the side of the building leading to the receiving docks. Most patrons chose to park closer to the various major entrances, so this location was remote. Virginia entered while the men settled back in the car with a six pack of beer to pass time.

Virginia walked around the various bars where patrons were playing video poker, sizing-up their appearance. She spotted a man later identified as Tony Franchetti, a local. Tony was in his mid-50s, overweight, slightly balding, and very well-dressed. He was wearing diamond rings on both hands. Virginia sat down and then intentionally dropped her coins on the bar and floor, letting out a little scream as she did so. Tony immediately helped her retrieve her money. She thanked him graciously and told him how glad she was that he was there and not someone else who may have kept some of her coins.

The conversation was warm and genuine. Tony enjoyed her company as they played. When Virginia ran out of coins, she said it wasn't her lucky night and she had to go.

"Wait, wait," said Tony, "take these and keep playing. Four aces are right around the corner for you."

At first she declined his generous offer, but he insisted. Virginia told Tony how nice he was, how nice he looked, and asked if he was with anyone that night. The conversation led to her inviting Tony to her apartment. He accepted. They left the casino. On the way to the car, Tony expressed surprise that Virginia would park in this area, suggesting he was becoming wary, but the two arrived at the car, as planned.

Both Ricky and Gary appeared and demanded Tony's money and jewelry. Tony was squeezed between the two on the side of the car and he reacted violently, pushing Gary to the pavement. Ricky panicked and shot Tony three times. Now all three were in a state of panic, and they jumped into the car and left the scene without so much as searching their victim for his money clip or wallet.

Tony Franchetti, a married man with four children and a successful real estate broker in the community, died on the dirty asphalt surface of the parking lot.

His surviving family filed a lawsuit against the hotel casino for inadequate security of the parking lots, which was a breach of duty because crime in parking lots was a known risk. I was retained by counsel representing the plaintiff.

The focus of my research was directed toward the frequency of criminal incidents in the parking areas of the complex, and the hotel's security strategy to provide adequate and reasonable protection for vehicles and patrons in those lots and ramps.

I concluded that the one officer dedicated to the exterior of the property for the purpose of patrolling all parking areas was inadequate—that is, with too much parking acreage and too many vehicles in a diversified pattern, one officer couldn't do the job alone.

I learned that one officer, assigned to the rear doors and dock, walked across the lot where this shooting occurred before the incident. He noted beer bottles on the pavement, one beer bottle sitting on the roof of a vehicle, and a young man seated on the hood of that vehicle drinking beer. Despite what he observed, he did not investigate or ask the young man what he was doing. He ignored this scene and continued on his way because parking lot problems were not part of his assignment. I told the jury if this officer had been properly trained he would have approached the young man sitting on the hood of the car and at least asked what he was doing, and why the bottles were scattered on the pavement. Had he done so, it could have scared off or otherwise spoiled the plan that was unfolding.

The expert for the hotel said he felt one exterior patrol was sufficient and drinking in public was legal in the state, as well as common practice, and to challenge and/or scold patrons was not the way the hotel and gaming industry operated.

The jury found for the hotel.

CHETIKOFF v. CITY BOWL

Edie Chetikoff and her husband, Ben, arrived at the parking lot with City Bowl on one end and K-Mart on the other, shortly before 5:00 p.m. They bowled every Thursday night in the Buck County League. League bowling started at 6:00 p.m. Both were wearing their bowling shirts, and they arrived early to warm-up and visit with long-time friends.

The bowling alley's front doors didn't face the street but, rather, faced the lot, in the direction of K-Mart, which faced the street. As they started toward the wide glass entry, Edie stopped and told Ben to go on in, that she wanted to run over to K-Mart to get a couple cartons of cigarettes. She'd meet him inside in a few minutes. Ben went ahead and Edie reversed her direction and walked over to the store.

It wasn't really dark yet, although the lot lights had come on, when Edie, with her purse in one hand and the sack containing cigarettes in the other, was heading back to the bowling alley. She was about a 150 feet from the entrance when suddenly and violently she felt her purse and arm being jerked by a young man. The sudden pulling caused her to fall and hit the parking lot surface where she broke her elbow and hip. The young man, running full speed and carrying the purse, disappeared among the autos parked in the lot. Edie shouted and tried to point in his direction but didn't see anyone chase the purse snatcher.

Someone called 9-1-1, and the police and an ambulance responded. Ben was summoned from the bowling alley and he ran to the lot still wearing his bowling shoes. Edie was taken to the hospital. While being placed on the gurney, a uniformed officer appeared among the spectators, and Ben asked him who he worked for.

"The bowling alley," responded the officer.

"Well," responded Ben, "where were you?" The officer then vanished from the somewhat hectic scene.

A lawsuit was filed against the bowling alley for inadequate security. Had the uniformed guard been at the front of City Bowl, as required, the purse snatcher would never have attacked Edie.

I was retained by the defense attorney to evaluate the incident and determine if the security was adequate or not. The primary focus of this evaluation had to do with the use and deployment of security personnel. The plaintiff's position was the guard wasn't on his post, which was right in front of the entrance to the bowling alley, and indeed he was not there.

I determined the schedule and assignment was as follows: Officer #1 reported for duty at 5:00 p.m. For the first half hour he was to station himself in front of the entrance, either out in the lot near the building, on the wide "porch" in front of the double glass doors, or just inside the glass doors. If requested, he would leave this area and assist or perform whatever he was asked. At about 5:30 p.m., he would conduct an exterior patrol around the entire building, returning to the front for another half hour. At about 9:30 p.m. he took a 30-minute break and was not relieved. At 10:00 p.m. he relieved Officer #2 for his 30-minute break.

Officer #2 reported for duty at 5:30 p.m., and his entire shift was devoted to the interior of the bowling alley, which included the inner lobby and desk area, arcade, cocktail lounge, dining room, and kitchen, checking the inner exterior doors and responding as required. At 9:30 p.m. he would go outside and relieve the officer assigned out there for 30 minutes.

A check of the daily reports and time cards revealed Officer #1 on the day of the incident had clocked-in at 5:03 p.m. Examination of months of time cards reflected a variation from 4:52 p.m. to 5:20 p.m. Examination of the daily security activity reports revealed there were times the first officer was called to attend to a task, such as overseeing the delivery door while it was open for a late delivery, immediately upon reporting for work, resulting in no security presence at the front.

The 9-1-1 record reflected the call was received at 5:09 p.m. During the deposition of Officer #1, the plaintiff's attorney, an aggressive and rather unpleasant man, determined the officer went to the bathroom immediately after clocking in.

I viewed the protection strategy as adequate. In fact, I thought it was most sufficient considering the nature of the business and the area of the county. And, in my opinion, the officer's presence or absence wasn't a factor in the crime. He wasn't assigned there for any specific task—it was only a starting point for the night's shift, and records established that.

During my deposition I felt the attorney for the plaintiff was "over the top" in his angry demeanor. I was there as an expert on security, and my evaluation was not to make a case in favor of the bowling alley, but simply present my opinion. Typically, attorneys on both sides are not happy with the opposite side's expert.

I testified the officer's presence or absence at that exact location wasn't a factor; even if he had been in front of building the event could have occurred, since he could have been inside, facing the opposite direction, or engaged in conversation. My conclusion was there was no liability. Nonetheless, the attorney hammered away at the issue, and got onto the fact the officer said he went into the restroom right after reporting for work. For some reason he was intent on this bathroom story and apparently didn't believe it.

I told him, "Mr. Sawyer, there are times when we all experience the need to go to the bathroom and go right *now!*"

He responded, "Not me. I was trained to hold it when I was in the military."

I said, "I can tell."

He literally jumped to his feet as though ready to punch me, and I too jumped up from my chair ready to engage if necessary. The attorney I was serving jumped to her feet to smooth the ruffled feathers and we all sat down and proceeded.

This case went to trial. Mr. Sawyer behaved nicely in front of the jury. The jury found for the bowling alley.

CHAPTER 13

A Summarization of Lawsuits That Were Rejected or Failed for Unusual Reasons

Contents

CASTENADA v. AMERICAN AVOCADO GROWERS

Eduardo Castenda was one of thousands of undocumented Mexican and Central American immigrants within 60 miles of the U.S. border, taking any kind of day-labor jobs he could find, and sending the bulk of his earnings back home to his wife and child in central Mexico.

As is common, these undocumented immigrants find each other and come together in small groups living in overly crowded houses rented by legal Mexican immigrants or, more often, camping in remote mountainous and rocky terrain, out of sight of busy highways and urban and suburban communities. They can be seen at the end of the day carrying plastic grocery bags containing beer and basic food supplies, disappearing into the dense countryside, heading for "home," a campsite without clean running water, power, or basic sanitation. Sometimes an immigrant woman or two share the camp. These people work in the dirt and sleep in the dirt, and their appearance gives them away as illegal day laborers.

Besides the natural need for companionship, these people come together for security purposes. Every day they can land a job is payday, in U.S. currency, and it accumulates fast before they can convert the cash into a money order and get it mailed off to Mexico. Safety in numbers is a survival strategy. Lone workers, even in the middle of the day, are frequently robbed by fellow immigrants. In the camps, each member of that community has a "secret" place he or she hides his or her money.

After several weeks in the United States, Eduardo made friends with three young men from his hometown, a natural common bond. The four of them moved away from an established camp and found a remote avocado grove that could only be reached by a rough dirt road almost a half-mile from any paved street. Each of the young men had an old bicycle to access the grove as well as to get to work. If selected to work for the day with some local rancher or party in need of labor, the employer-for-the-day would throw their bikes into the back of his or her truck and off they'd go.

The grove had no power but did have irrigation piping that they tapped into, illegally, for fresh water. So housekeeping was set up on trespassed land.

The four, when not working as day laborers, constructed a "house" comprised of pieces of heavy cardboard cartons, sheets of corrugated tin, plastic and vinyl sheets, and plywood and other wood scraps salvaged from the surrounding areas. It even had a padlock to secure the door on the outside when they weren't home, and the same lock was used on the inside when they slept at night. It was a pretty flimsy arrangement but it provided some protection against the rain and cold nights and provided each man with his own space.

No other undocumented immigrants knew of this new camp, nor did local residents who lived on the far side of the grove.

One Saturday morning Eduardo and one companion rode close to town, hid their bikes in the bushes, and walked to the local weekend swap meet. While browsing through the various vendor's wares and booths, they met two fellow countrymen from their hometown in Mexico, who, according to them, had been in the general area a couple of years. They were sharply dressed, well groomed, wearing new lizard-skin cowboy boots and white hats, and had nicely trimmed black moustaches. There was much back-slapping and handshaking between the four, despite the sharp contrast between the appearance of Eduardo and his friend compared to the other men.

After visiting and sharing stories and news from home, Carlos, the apparent leader of the two, said he had a nice car and asked Eduardo and his friend if they would like a ride home. Eduardo was proud to show off his camp and the four drove to the edge of the paved road and walked the rest of the way into the grove. Carlos was most complimentary over the "house" and site selection. They all had a shot of tequila as they sat under the avocado trees, then returned toward town, where Carlos dropped off the two to retrieve their bicycles. They all agreed to meet again at the swap meet around noon the next Saturday.

The chance meeting was a pleasant surprise and all four sat around the fire that evening and talked about home and some of the news they had learned that day. Around midnight, the door of the little shack burst open with a deafening crash, when kicked in by the largest of four dark figures, indistinguishable because of the total darkness of the location, and the sleepers were immediately attacked, beaten, and stabbed. The entire shack was destroyed and collapsed, and the money of each laborer was either found or was given up by its beaten owner.

Eduardo was stabbed in the skull. The knife remained lodged in his head with the handle protruding.

The least injured man ran wildly through the grove where he knew he could locate a house and seek help.

Nearby residents were awakened, and they called the police. There was difficulty in finding the site of the crime. When the police were guided there, they radioed for an air medevac to get Eduardo to the hospital's emergency room and trauma team. Eduardo was in intensive care for weeks, but he survived.

Once released, Eduardo obtained the services of a Mexican-American attorney in town whose practice was exclusively for the Mexican community. On Eduardo's behalf, he filed a lawsuit against the owners of the avocado grove, as well as the contractor who managed the grove. Their complaint alleged the management company's grove supervisor knew they were living there and was collecting rent from the four, under the table. Therefore, as lawful tenants who paid their rent regularly, they were not trespassers, and they were entitled to a reasonable level of security, but none was provided. They also alleged the grove should have been enclosed by cyclone fencing to keep intruders out and some lighting should have been provided inside the grove.

I was retained by the law firm representing the owner of the grove and the grove management company.

The plaintiff retained an expert, a security consultant I knew, who inspected the property the same day I was there. We greeted each other but otherwise did not discuss the matter. I suspect he was as appalled by the filth of the campsite as I was. Trash littered the area and no one location was designated for latrine purposes. I understood he had already formed his opinion and was in agreement with the plaintiff's theory of liability.

The grove manager, a legal Mexican immigrant, had quit his job prior to the incident and could not be located. In my view, even if he could have been found and even if he admitted collecting (or extorting) "rent," he was not acting within the scope of his employment, and he was not empowered to charge or collect rent, and there was no duty owed to the trespassers.

For comparison purposes I surveyed the many avocado groves for miles around and only a fraction were enclosed with fencing. None had lights inside the grove.

I testified in deposition as to my opinion about the grove manager's role, if indeed it was true, as well as my findings of comparable properties, and opined there was no duty to provide security nor was there a breach of duty.

Based on the opinions and the summary of the case, the defense filed a motion for summary judgment and the court dismissed the case.

HUNT v. J. J. STORES

J.J. Stores was a five-and-dime. They normally did not have a security employee, but they did hire a part-time off-duty policeman during the holidays. Two days before Christmas, Mr. and Mrs. Hunt, quite elderly senior citizens, went to the store, more for something to do than to actually shop. Mrs. Hunt had all her faculties, but her husband was showing signs of dementia. He followed her wherever she went, and on this occasion was following her as she wandered through the store. Officer Howard Cones was on duty as security for the store and noticed the couple. He decided to follow them because the old man put his hands on everything. In the children's department he observed the old man take a boy's belt from a rack and stick it under his sweater. Mrs. Hunt was unaware of what her husband had done. They eventually left the store with Cones in pursuit.

Out on the crowded sidewalk, Cones made the decision to retrieve the belt before stopping them and identifying himself. From behind Mr. Hunt he reached over the man's shoulder and into the partially buttoned cardigan sweater and pulled out the belt. Mr. Hunt cried out in surprise, which caused Mrs. Hunt to immediately turn around and see a stranger in a brown sweater, Cones, with his arm draped over her husband's shoulder. Thinking the man was a robber, she whirled about, reached over her husband, and scratched the officer's face.

Mr. Hunt was arrested on the scene for shoplifting and his wife was arrested for felonious assault of a police officer, a serious crime. They were handcuffed and marched to the basement of the store to the security office and then rehandcuffed to a pipe about shoulder high.

Common practice in the city mandated the issuance of a citation for the minor crime of shoplifting and prompt release. People weren't taken to jail anymore unless the charge was considered a felony. However, Cones was upset with being scratched and called his station requesting a unit be dispatched to the store to transport his prisoners and book them into the city jail. Because it was a busy season, no police unit could make it to the store for over three hours.

The district attorney's office recommended to the court the dismissal of the criminal charges "in the interest of justice" considering the advanced age of the offenders and the value of the boy's belt.

I was retained by the attorney representing the couple in the civil action for unlawful and excessive use of force. The attorney said he was working hard to get a trial as quickly as possible because Mr. Hunt was nearing the end of his life. Before the trial could be set, Mr. Hunt died.

As an expert in shoplifting, I considered Cones' handling of this incident outrageous, in terms of his recovering the belt, chaining older people to a pipe for three hours, locking them up, and filing a felonious assault on the wife.

The trial was subsequently set. As it approached, the attorney was worried Mrs. Hunt too would pass away and that would end the case (my case too, because I was prepared to inform the jury how badly this whole matter had been handled and how the police department, if they wanted their officers to work shoplifting, should provide some training). The attorney also said his client was becoming very difficult to deal with. Mrs. Hunt was especially cranky and was getting reluctant to proceed with the trial.

At the end of the first day of trial, the attorney phoned me with an incredulous story. He told me that in the morning, during the selection of the jury, Mrs. Hunt, who was seated at the counsel table with him, said in a clear, loud voice, "I don't want no blacks on my jury!" The African-American judge and the two African-American jurors already seated in the jury box didn't blink, but everyone knew this was a "fatal" remark. The full jury was quickly seated and the trial process beat all-time records. The matter was decided, in favor of J. J. Stores, before the day was over. The attorney called it the most accelerated trial in the state's history, short of hanging horse thieves in the last century.

That concluded my expert witness assignment.

JACKSON v. NATIONAL DISCOUNTERS

"Sonny" Jackson only caught the loss prevention agent's attention because of his size. This was a large man indeed. Agent Bud Hovley thought he might be a professional football player, a lineman perhaps, as he followed the customer in the store, more out of curiosity than suspicion. And then, in the costume jewelry area, to the agent's amazement, the man openly placed one inexpensive watch on his left wrist and stuck a second watch in his right front pocket without any apparent concern anyone may have been watching. The customer then reversed his direction and headed toward the garden department and its exit door to the parking lot.

Two reactions raced through Hovley's mind: good, I've got myself a shoplifter, and bad, how can I possibly arrest this man, if he resists? As he followed the customer he signaled to the garden department manager to call for help and follow him to assist, if needed. The manager acknowledged the signal.

Sonny left the store and Hovley was satisfied the six steps required for a shoplifting arrest had been met: (1) see the customer approach the merchandise, (2) see the customer select the merchandise, (3) see the customer conceal the goods, (4) maintain an uninterrupted surveillance to ensure against the merchandise being discarded, put back, or paid for, (5) see that the customer does not pay for the item, and (6) stop the customer once he or she exits the store. Hovley was now outside gaining ground as Jackson reached his car and started opening the door.

"Excuse me, sir. I'm with National Discounters, and you have merchandise you did not pay for."

Sonny released the door handle, removed the watch from his wrist, and handed it to Hovley. "You're right, I'm sorry," he said and turned to continue opening the door to his vehicle.

"And the other watch, the one in your pocket?" asked the agent.

Sonny surrendered the second watch and again tried to fully open the car's door. Hovely held his hand against the door and told the customer he had to return to the store to finalize this matter. By now the garden manager and a stock boy were on the scene, standing behind Hovely.

Sonny shoved Hovely, and the agent, a former police officer, seized the big man's arm resulting in the two tumbling to the ground. Hovely shouted for help and the two store employees joined in the struggle on the pavement. A customer passing by shouted for someone to call the sheriff. Customers in the fast-food restaurant nearby watched the group of men struggling, and an employee also called the sheriff.

It was apparent Sonny was not going to willingly submit, was profane, and threatening those who were on top of him, and was struggling desperately to get upright and to his feet. Hovley was afraid the man could easily injure him as well as the others and was intent on holding the man down on the surface of the lot until the sheriff deputies arrived. Another customer, realizing the difficulty the store employees were having, joined in and he too helped hold down Sonny.

In the distance sirens could be heard and two sheriff units arrived and pulled the men a part, handcuffed Sonny, and took him to the county jail. En route to jail, Sonny complained his shoulder and legs were "on fire" and asked for medical attention. The jail's booking office wouldn't accept the prisoner until he received medical attention, so Sonny was transported to the local emergency room where burns on his body were treated.

Sonny was charged in the local court with misdemeanor theft, pled guilty, and paid a small fine. Subsequently, he obtained the services of an attorney who filed a lawsuit against the store claiming excessive use of force.

I was retained by the store as their expert. In my review of the incident in its entirety, the complaint alleged it was unreasonable and excessive to hold down the man on the hot black macadam surface of the lot. The language of the complaint included the fact that on this particular summer day the local temperature was 107 degrees and the superheated surface of the lot caused severe burns and scarring to the plaintiff's body. This conduct, on the part of the employees, was cruel and unnecessary.

After reviewing the materials, including the photographs of the burns that would be introduced as evidence during the trial, the defense attorney and I discussed the case. I told him there was some merit in the complaint, considering the temperature, and said the whole matter could have been averted if the agent had handcuffed the man while they had him immobilized on the ground.

I was informed the agent didn't have handcuffs that day, and when I asked why not, I learned the regional loss prevention manager had sent out an order prohibiting their use for 30 days as a form of "punishment" because one agent had abused their use.

As we sat there in his office I stated the following:

While I'm testifying, if Jackson's attorney asks me, "Mr. Sennewald, you're a recognized expert in matters connected with shoplifting including people who are arrested but are afraid to go to jail and sometimes resist. Correct?" And I'd agree. And if the attorney continues and asks, "If the store's security agent had handcuffed my client, Mr. Jackson, and lifted him off the pavement to his feet, that would have been custom and practice in the industry, isn't that correct?" And I'd agree. And if he pursued that line of questioning he'd most likely ask me if that's the course of action I would recommend, as an expert and consultant, and I'd answer yes. Then he'd certainly ask me if, in my investigation into this event, I inquired why his client wasn't handcuffed and lifted off the pavement, I would be bound to answer, "I did inquire," and he'd ask, "What did you learn?" I would be bound to reply the agent wasn't allowed to carry his handcuffs that day because of a ban imposed by a supervisor as punitive action because some agent in some store misused his handcuffs.

The store's attorney knew what I knew: my answer would infuriate the jury and they would find for the plaintiff. The store's attorney would lose his case.

But we both also knew that an expert witness, any witness for that matter, must only answer the questions that are asked by counsel, or by the court (judge). Put another way, witnesses may not or should not volunteer information or answer questions that are not propounded by counsel.

That key question was not asked during my deposition nor during the trial.

I testified in the trial that the store personnel and a helpful customer were all concerned for their safety because Sonny, a very large man, was threatening and they collectively were afraid to let this man up and suffer the consequences.

The jury found for the store.

Had the attorney representing Sonny asked the "right" question, I suspect the trial would have had an entirely different outcome. Was justice served?

UNIVERSAL INSURANCE CO. v. GOLD SHIELD SECURITY SERVICES

Northern Mills was a major lumber company surrounded by a majestic forest. It was one of many lumber operations in the area, and the community's economy was solely dependent on lumber products and related services. Northern Mills' insurance carrier was Universal Insurance Company.

Security was not viewed so much as a crime prevention effort as much as it was a fire prevention activity, and every mill had active programs to prevent as well as fight fires on their various properties.

Northern Mills had a small staff of security officers whose primary and most important task was to patrol the property at night and on weekends and holidays as a "fire watch." One of the guards retired, leaving a vacancy, and every effort to replace him failed. That vacancy created an added payroll expense because overtime was required to cover his shift, midnight to seven in the morning.

To resolve this dilemma, Mike Poole, Northern Mills' superintendent, phoned Gold Shield Security Services to come out and discuss providing an officer to fill the vacancy. Gold Shield's account manager, Bill Husk, met with Mike and they walked the property and discussed the terms of a contract that would be satisfactory to both parties. The contract for services detailed, in clear language, what the arrangements were, how problems would be solved, how to resolve differences, and the cost for one security officer who would be dedicated to this property. Three days after both parties signed the contract, Henry "Hank" MacIntosh reported to Mike at the designed place and time and commenced his first graveyard shift working on-the-job training alongside a current security officer named Phil Gardner.

The task was relatively simple. The officer carried a "time clock," a specifically designed clock with a replaceable paper disk that fit in the mechanism, the face of which rotated around inside reflecting the hours and minutes in synch with the clock. The clock was encased in a leather case with a shoulder strap for ease of carrying all night. The route the guard was to follow had been established for years; the guard's job was to follow the route and at designated locations along the way remove a key, chained to a small metal box secured to a building or any object, insert the key with a number on the edge of the key into a slot in the time clock, turn the key, and the number would be physically embossed on the paper disk.

Therefore, when the guard visited the pump house and keyed that station, which was designated as station 11, a supervisor's examination of the embossed numbers of the paper disk the next morning would reveal that station 11 was visited at, for example, 12:43 a.m., 1:59 a.m., 3:07 a.m., etc.

This was a supervisorial tool to ensure the guard was indeed walking and working rather than sitting in his car taking a nap. If he did take a nap, theoretically the supervisor should detect it by the unexplained absence of "station hits" for any given period of time. Along the route were emergency phones and firefighting equipment that was explained and could be used temporarily until the fire department from town could reach the scene.

Several months into the job a major fire broke out at Northern Mills on Hank's shift. It was a huge loss. Arson investigators were confident it was intentionally set and were suspicious Hank was the culprit, but they didn't have sufficient evidence to charge him formally with the crime. Investigators from the state as well as the insurance company questioned

Hank but he denied setting the fire. The matter went unsolved. An insurance claim was filed.

The insurance carrier, Universal Insurance, filed a lawsuit against Gold Shield Security Services complaining their security officer was negligent and, had he followed instructions, he could have minimized the fire, therefore his negligence was the cause of the loss. Not only was Hank negligent in not being timely in responding to the fire, he had been negligent in hitting his time clock stations regularly, and that failure pointed to the fact he wasn't where he should have been when the fire broke out.

I was retained by the law firm representing Gold Shield, and was provided with the typical boxes of documents for my inspection and review. Among the material were the time clock disks for the graveyard shift for one year up to and including the night of the fire.

Following my investigation I met with the attorneys in this multimillion-dollar lawsuit and after some preliminary small talk about the flight and weather, they asked how my review went and what I thought.

I said, "Gentlemen, I have good news and bad news."

"Why don't you give us the bad news first?" said the lead attorney.

"My opinion agrees with the suspicion of the earlier investigators; your guy, Hank, set the fire."

"Oh great! What could the good news possibly be, in view of that?"

I explained that the good news was that it really was not important whether Hank set the fire or not for the following reason: The typical security service contract is pretty much "boilerplate," including the language the officer will be checked X number of times during his or her shift by a guard company supervisor, like a sergeant, lieutenant, or captain, who oversees an area within which the guard company has personnel posted. That means the supervisor drives from location to location at all hours and makes a spot-check to ensure the guard isn't sleeping or otherwise is alert. Also, a typical contract requires the guard to submit a copy of what is called a DAR (daily activity report) to the client and to the guard company office for their review and inspection, another supervisorial tool to ensure the work is being done as required. That language was removed from the Northern Mills contract, by Northern Mills.

So, what was important here was not what the language of the contract said, but what it didn't say, and the consequences of that. In this case it means Northern Mills did not want their contracted guard supervised by the guard company; they relieved the guard company of their normal supervisorial duty to check on and supervise the guard assigned to their property and, as a consequence, the guard was a de facto employee of Northern Mills, not the guard company's employee. The guard service simply provided a person for them to use as they saw fit.

A careful examination of the daily time clock disks told me Northern Mills didn't really inspect them and had they done so, they would have seen numerous failures to patrol as required by the absence of station hits. Northern Mills was responsible for Hank's performance, good or bad. I concluded, "The security service cannot be held liable, in my opinion, for someone's performance if they have no control over the employee."

The matter settled.[*]

HENDERSON v. VALLEY MALL

During the holiday season the enclosed Valley Mall located in the north-eastern United States closed at 10:00 p.m. Parking in the huge surface lot that surrounded the mall accommodated approximately 5,000 parking spaces. Overnight parking in the lot was not allowed. The weather was light snow and the temperature registered an overnight low of 15 degrees. Only two mall security officers were on duty between 11:00 p.m. and 7:00 a.m. Their task was to patrol the property that, on this shift, was divided into two zones, the interior of the shopping center and the exterior parking lot.

The interior officer's task was to walk the enclosed mall, ensure the various merchant's doors were secure, and view the interior of each store alert for anything unusual, such as a possible fire or water flow from faulty sprinklers, an intruder, or someone left locked inside. It wasn't common, but from time to time people had either fallen asleep or passed out and later found themselves locked in a relatively dark department store.

That interior officer would note the time he commenced his rounds and make notations of anything unusual, for example, "03:31 a.m., noted padlock not locked on accordion gate in front of Snuffy's Sporting Goods big window. Checked interior with flashlight. I snapped the lock shut. Nothing unusual noted." At the conclusion of the officer's rounds he would note the time on the activity log.

The exterior officer was required to circle the property once an hour, being alert to any activity outside, such as a gathering of vehicles driven by juveniles, drag racing, abandoned vehicles, checking the exterior gates that

---

[*] More often than not, the expert witness is not informed of the details of a settlement. Actually, the settlement is none of the expert's business, and I personally have never sought clarification of the outcome of a case.

led to the store's receiving dock areas, check for burned-out lamps on the many parking light stanchions and note their location for the maintenance department, and any other observation or event worthy of his attention and action, such as an early callout for the snow-removal team, if warranted, and enter his activity and actions on the activity log. The last parking lot patrol for this graveyard shift was scheduled at 6:00 a.m.

By 7:00 a.m. each morning the activity common to large shopping centers was underway, including cleaning crews arriving, trash trucks, early deliveries for any number of stores, and various employees with other early-morning duties to prepare for the coming business day.

The security day shift now increased to full staffing, the interior of the mall was increased to the full four patrol zones, plus the dispatcher, supervisor, director of security, and two exterior officers, one of whom did the first day shift parking lot patrol at about 7:30 a.m.

On this December morning at about 10:00 a.m. a customer contacted a security officer in the mall and reported a strange sight in the parking lot—a parked vehicle dusted with snow from earlier in the morning and a woman with her leg up on the dash. Security officers responded to the location and found a dead woman seated in her auto. A subsequent police investigation revealed she had been stabbed to death.

As a consequence, a civil lawsuit was filed against Valley Mall for negligent security, alleging the shopping center was a known dangerous location and the security provided was inadequate. I was retained by the law firm defending the mall.

In reviewing the defendant's "answer to the complaint" (the allegations reflected in the preceding paragraph), I noted the defense denied the mall was a "known dangerous area," that it had an unusually low frequency of crime against property, and crimes against persons were rare. The defendant contended its proximity to a nearby private university campus and small-town community both with low crime rates represented a relatively safe environment, and the number of security officers was in keeping with comparable regional shopping centers.

My task was to independently confirm this information, as well as all the facts and circumstances surrounding this event.

My research into the history of criminal incidents on the premises as well as the crime rates for the greater area verified they were indeed low, lower than average for comparable geographical settings.

My review of the local police department's crime report and subsequent investigation revealed a college student had bled to death after being stabbed while seated in her car. The time of the stabbing and exact time of death could not be fixed. The curious and quite startling information in the investigator's report was the dead woman; when the police arrived some minutes after 10:00 a.m., was frozen stiff!

The question in my mind from my perspective, as well as in the homicide detective's mind from his perspective, was: When was she stabbed and when did she expire? His perspective, naturally, had to do with identifying the murderer and his motive, and mine was how long did it take for the victim to bleed to death, and once she expired while dressed warmly inside of a vehicle, how long would it take for her to freeze solid? And even more important, to me, was how could the patrol officers, doing their hourly patrol, not find her? Was it possible they could have found her on the first patrol around 11:00 p.m. and saved her life? Or even the midnight round?

Examination of the security officer's log sheet, reflecting the hourly entries of patrols and observations, disclosed the two officers alternated the patrols—that is, Robert Jones patrolled inside the mall while Gene Miller did the exterior patrol. Therefore, the log reflected "Jones to outside patrol, 2303 (military time for 11:03 p.m.) and rounds completed 2341 all okay."; "Miller outside patrol 0005 and rounds completed 0030, all okay." And so the notations went, hour by hour.

I decided to identify the kind of patrol vehicle these officers were provided for this outside work in subfreezing weather and asked for the security vehicle patrol and maintenance reports. Maybe the vehicle's heater didn't work and the officers hurried through their patrol because it was so cold outside. I was also curious how many miles the officers put on the vehicle as evidenced by the daily odometer readings. The readings would help me calculate the number of times the vehicle circled and crisscrossed this exceptionally large property's footprint.

I was informed the management of the center had decided to eliminate the vehicle so as to reduce operating expenses. The officers, as a consequence, were required to walk in that weather. I formed the opinion they did not walk; they did not patrol; they did not see that lone vehicle sitting there all night, because they refused to go out in the cold just to save the company money, right or wrong. They falsified their daily log and were never checked to ensure they were doing their job as expected.

More often than not I interview the officers involved in a case for the benefit of their explanation. In this case, irrespective of their statements, even if they told me they diligently walked the perimeter, they couldn't explain to my satisfaction why they did not check the lone vehicle, relatively close to the main entrance, and check the interior. The failure was twofold: management denying the officers a basic tool for the job and the officers' failure to investigate the vehicle (if they did go outside), which would fall below the acceptable standards of a professional security officer.

But for the poor management decision to take away the officers' patrol vehicle, therefore forcing them to walk in freezing and inclement weather, the victim of that stabbing may have survived her wounds.

In my professional opinion the protection program for that property was not adequate and the performance fell below the standard of care. I informed the defense firm I was unable to continue assisting them in their defense of the mall and they would be obliged to find another security expert.

OLEA v. THE CLEVELAND HOTEL

The Cleveland Hotel was considered a major landmark in the downtown area of a major Midwestern city. It was constructed at the turn of the twentieth century, 11 stories high, red brick, classic canopy over the wide glass door entry facing Main Street, with a secondary entrance with a porte-cochere on the west side of the building staffed with a tall, handsome, elegantly dressed doorman in period attire. As automobiles became the main mode of transportation the porte-cochere was the natural entrance for arrivals and departures and for valet parking. The main entrance on Main Street was a pedestrian entrance into a grand high-ceiling atrium. Registered guests and visitors preferred to use the main entrance if not using their automobile.

Security personnel were part of the staff. Traditional deployment of officers was as follows:

- Post #1: one officer was assigned to the roving patrol of the upper floors for security and fire watch purposes.
- Post #2: one officer was assigned to oversee the general porte-cochere area, the arrival and departure of guests, and make infrequent checks of the parking garage.
- Post #3: one officer was assigned to patrol the main floor of the hotel and monitor the lobby area and oversee traffic coming and going through the main entrance and main lobby.
- Post #4: one officer was to serve as relief for lunch and coffee breaks of the other three officers.

The officers were so deployed for three shifts a day, 365 days a year. When special events were held at the hotel and when the annual parade occurred on Main Street, the staff was augmented with extra uniformed officers contracted from an outside guard service.

Jorge and Maria Olea and Maria's brother and sister-in-law, Ricardo and Elena Sepulveda, were guests in town, celebrating Maria's 60th birthday. Across the street and kitty-corner from the hotel was a plaza with fountains, flower beds, winding walkways all beautifully illuminated at night, and especially so during this time, the Christmas season. It was a popular attraction for guests to the city, as well as locals.

But there was a dark side to the park—the persistent presence of homeless street people and occasional drunks wandering in the area. The old hotel's neighbors had deteriorated over time and were on the verge of becoming a skid row. The city decided to clean up the area, modernize it, and put in the plaza. Some dingy and empty buildings remained but were not as noticeable as in the past. Yet it was still an attractive tourist area.

On the second night of the Oleas' and Sepulvedas' stay, they decided to visit the plaza, enjoy the Christmas decorations, and perhaps visit some of the shops on the backside of the gardens.

Upon returning they crossed the two streets to reach the front entrance of the hotel and entered the hotel, at about 9:00 p.m. The vast lobby area was empty of guests. As they proceeded through the lobby, unknown to them, a "street person" had followed them in and stealthily approached the two couples from behind. He grabbed Maria's handbag and forcibly ribbed it away from her grasp—a classic "purse snatch." The force used in the event caused Maria to fall, breaking her hip.

Jorge went to the aid of his wife. Ricardo gave chase but couldn't catch the fleeing robber. Maria was taken to the hospital in an ambulance and major hip surgery was required, ending the holiday trip.

The Oleas obtained legal counsel and a lawsuit was filed against the hotel for inadequate security. They contended had there been a security officer monitoring traffic in and out of the main entrance, this event would not have happened. The hotel's position was the security staff was adequate and the small amount of traffic in and out of the main lobby and main front doors didn't warrant or justify an officer's permanent presence.

The filing of the lawsuit was processed to the hotel's insurance carrier who in turn designated a well-established and experienced law firm to handle the defense. The attorney assigned to that case retained me to evaluate the claim and the security program and assist in the defense.

My assessment disclosed that within the year prior to the Oleas' and Sepulvedas' visit the hotel was purchased by a foreign investor. New ownership invariably brings changes. One change included reducing the security budget. The new budget reduced the staff from four officers to three—that is, post #1 remained the same and post #3 was eliminated, and posts #2 and #4 were combined with infrequent checks of the main entrance.

I contacted the attorney I was assisting and told him the revised and reduced security arrangement was inadequate, that the main floor, main atrium, and front doors were not adequately covered, and I was unable to testify in the defense of the hotel. In my view the attorney, a respected member of the local bar association, knew that the protection was inadequate and may have argued the matter with the insurance adjuster, but proceeded as he should as an attorney. I'm confident he knew what my opinion would be and the case would go away (settle). He thanked me for my opinion and said he'd call me back. Later that day he called and said the insurance adjuster wanted a three-way telephone conference so we could discuss this further. The call was scheduled.

During that call I personally told the adjuster the security coverage was inadequate and the main floor and entrance was a risk area and required more coverage. The adjuster said he didn't agree and wanted me to reassess my position. I said there was nothing further for me to analyze or review and I was satisfied the case was not defensible, or at least I couldn't contribute. I wouldn't risk my reputation by testifying security was adequate when I knew it wasn't. He insisted the case was defensible, and I said to him, "Who's the expert, you or me? I'm telling you the security was inadequate, and as a consequence of poor coverage the plaintiff in this case was criminally victimized and injured. If you want me to testify for you, that's what I will tell the jury."

My services ended. Although I wasn't so informed, I'm confident they settled the matter and the former guest was compensated; unless, of course, the defense firm was obliged to go out and find another "expert" who would testify in support of the insurance adjuster's opinions. And that happens!

HESTON v. BIG GRAND STORES

Store policy required employees to park on the perimeter of the store's vast parking lot, a common practice in shopping center and box store operations, so as to ensure customers have preferential parking close to the store.

A young man, Anthony Sims, was initially seen in the morning around 9:30 a.m. near a 24-hour fast-food restaurant, on the edge of the store's parking lot. He was seen on the lot and in the store at various hours all day and evening. At midnight, an employee, Becky Heston, clocked out and walked to her truck across the lot, followed by this young man. As she opened the door of her vehicle Anthony surprised her, forced her across the cab to the passenger's side, and drove her to a remote location.

There was a loss prevention agent on duty inside the store, whose primary task was to detect shoplifters as well as handle other types of criminal offenses, such as use of stolen credit cards and the passing of worthless bank checks.

The store and the parking lot was equipped with over 100 "fixed" CCTV cameras, meaning each was focused on a given area and could not be panned or tilted remotely to follow anyone or change the direction in which the camera was aimed. All the cameras were recorded around the clock.

The parking lot was patrolled by a contracted security service that provided a uniformed officer and patrol vehicle with distinctive markings and flashing yellow lights mounted on the roof. In keeping with the request of store management, this vehicle was in constant use, patrolling up and down isles and circling the lot so as to create a security presence.

At 12:30 a.m. Becky's sister called the store, inquiring if her sister was still working, and if not, what time did she leave the store? Becky should have arrived home by 12:15 a.m. The assistant manager confirmed Becky had left the store a couple minutes after her shift at 12:02 a.m. and the sister should be patient and allow a little more time. Surely Becky would arrive any minute now.

Anthony Sims parked the truck in a remote area not far from the store and raped Becky after forcing her to undress. Following that first rape she was allowed to redress. Anthony then drove her to his parents' mobile home located on a tract of farm land, devoid of any nearby homes. He cautioned Becky not to cry-out or awaken his mother if she didn't want to be hurt. He then raped her in his own bed. Anthony's mother was asleep in her bedroom and his father was working the graveyard shift. He wasn't due home until about 8:00 a.m.

At 12:50 a.m., Becky's sister called the store again and had the assistant manager paged. She was truly alarmed and asked him to have someone check to see if Becky's truck was parked in the employee parking area. It was not. She said she was going to call the police and report

Becky missing. At that moment a local police officer arrived at the store for a cup of coffee. The assistant manager put the police officer on the phone.

The officer took the "missing person" report, which included Becky's description and the description of her truck. The officer asked if the camera system viewed the employee parking area and if the store agent could bring the image up on a monitor. The agent on duty at that time couldn't do that, but the assistant store manager called the senior agent at home and asked him to come to the store to assist. Time was passing.

At about 3:00 a.m., Anthony ushered Becky out of the trailer, put her in the truck, and drove on the interstate, crossing into the next state. He stopped for gas and searched her purse for money to pay for the gas and some "munchies." A cheap motel was nearby, so Anthony rented a room. Once in the room, Becky was allowed to shower and was then raped again. At no time did she resist his sexual demands out of fear for her life.

While the abductor and victim were at the hotel, the senior agent was at the security camera counsel and had the cameras on the east side of the store rolled back to midnight. The monitors replayed the recordings as the assistant store manager, police officer, and two loss prevention agents watched. They observed Becky walking from the employee door diagonally across the lot, followed by a male figure some 50 feet behind her, only closing the gap as she approached and opened the door to the truck. They saw the blur of movement ending with the man seated behind the steering wheel backing out of the parking slip and then driving out of the lot on the road headed toward the interstate. Becky's head was barely visible on the passenger's side. They had just witnessed an abduction four hours after the fact. By this time Becky's sister had dressed and drove to the store. She was informed of their findings.

An "all-points" broadcast was made to law enforcement agencies, including the license plate number of the truck.

At daybreak Anthony decided to return his home. He put Becky back in the passenger's seat. Some 40 miles from the state line he pulled the truck off the interstate onto a construction site, drove less than 50 feet from the interstate, behind a pile of dirt, and murdered Becky. After shooting her in the head and face, Anthony drove back onto the interstate headed toward home. He realized he had spent all of Becky's money, so he decided to rob the very gas station he had stopped at earlier using the same gun he had just used to kill Becky. As he left the gas station, stuffing the bills into his pockets, a state trooper pulled into the lot. Anthony stood there, gun in hand, and surrendered. He took the troopers back to the scene of the shooting and to the motel. It was now about 9:00 a.m. and the criminal matter was relatively resolved.

The family wasted no time obtaining counsel who filed a civil action against the store as well as the security contract service for inadequate security and negligence. They also obtained the services of two security experts.

Those plaintiff experts viewed hours of videotapes, reviewed the store's loss prevention policies and program, and scrutinized the contract between the store and the security service company, including the post orders. The post orders were professionally crafted and obviously based on years of experience between the two parties. The experiences and events that drive the language of post orders are typically based on a history of failures or criminal events.

The plaintiff's conclusion and opinion was the store and guard company were negligent in terms of allowing Anthony to loiter on and around the store for 14 and a half hours, despite signage and a policy prohibiting loitering. They opined, had Anthony been properly challenged, such challenging would either have discouraged or frightened him to go elsewhere. Absent such aggressive challenges, they pointed to the various videotapes that, over a span of hours, especially after dark, showed Anthony sitting on the bus bench near one of the stores main entrances, and he followed various young women as they walked out to their vehicles, but reversed his direction when he saw the security vehicle with its flashing lights approaching or nearby. Clearly, they said, he was picking potential victims but was deterred by the constant patrol.

Therefore, the plaintiff's position was the patrol officer's failure to either ask the young man to leave the property if he had no intention of shopping or bringing the matter to the attention of his supervisor, a specific member of store management on duty, and such failure contributed to Anthony's eventual success of following and kidnapping a victim.

I was retained by counsel for both defendants. I, of course, reviewed the same material examined by the plaintiff's experts.

My review of the hours of videotapes and reading of contracts, policies, and history of events on the property disclosed four interesting points that buttressed the defendant's position they were indeed not negligent in making the property reasonably safe against foreseeable events. The defendants felt their notice and challenges satisfied a reasonable security awareness and response to Anthony's presence.

1. Anthony approached a store supervisor and security officer, Dan Stanley, out in the lot near the fast-food restaurant around noon, asking directions to one of the nearby interstate highways, so he had eye contact and a verbal exchange with representatives of the store.

2. Anthony was observed sitting on the bench mid-afternoon and Officer Stanley, having seen the young man on the property for several hours, dismounted from his patrol vehicle, approached Anthony, and asked him what he was doing. Anthony replied he was waiting for a friend to pick him up. "Where's your friend coming from?" asked the officer. "Over by Lockwood," responded Anthony, "and he should be here soon." Satisfied, Officer Stanley then commented on the weather and continued on his patrol. Clearly, Officer Stanley was observant and took reasonable action to inquire and make his presence known.

3. Around 10:00 p.m. the assistant store manager came out of the store for a cigarette and observed Anthony on the bench. Thinking Anthony was an employee on a break, he asked him where he worked. "I don't work here," he replied, "I'm just waiting for a ride." Officer Stanley saw the two sitting on the bench but had no idea as to their conversation. So this was the third contact with a representative of the store, but Anthony apparently didn't feel he was arousing any suspicion.

4. Around 11:15 p.m. Officer Stanley had to get out of his jeep to tell a customer he was double parked and had to move. While standing by his vehicle he again observed Anthony on the bench and walked over to him. "You sure someone's coming for you buddy?" he asked, indicating he was clearly aware of Anthony's continued presence on the property. "Yes sir, coming right soon," replied Anthony. There was a pause, Anthony did not turn to face or look at Officer Stanley during this exchange, and Officer Stanley shrugged and accepted the answer, returning to his vehicle and continuing his patrol.

The issue was, what more could the security officer have done and was he in compliance with his post orders? The post orders clearly stated that the outside patrol officer did not have the authority to eject or trespass any loiters or suspicious or rowdy persons, such as a group of juveniles gathering on the property, but he was required to report those conditions or any other unusual or suspicious circumstances to a member of store management and that management person would take appropriate action.

In my view, Officer Stanley failed to comprehend the importance of Anthony's answering his question without looking at him, despite the fact Officer Stanley thought that was peculiar. In view of the totality of circumstances of the long day, the officer should have followed his instructions and simply called his supervisor (the very store management employee who sat on the bench with Anthony) and requested a brief meeting to share a concern. When the supervisor came out Officer Stanley would have reported that this young man had been on the property all day, and had twice said he was waiting for a ride, the first time at allegedly at 3:30 p.m. and again just now, but the young man wouldn't look him in the eye when asked about that ride again. The supervisor would have investigated by approaching Anthony and most likely would have been even more suspicious, considering the amount of time he'd been there. He would have either offered to phone his friend with the car or suggest he go down to the gas station and wait there. In my view, the store supervisor's presence and questions would have alarmed Anthony, discouraged his intentions, and he would have moved on. Had he left the property, Becky would not have been followed to her truck, abducted, raped, and murdered.

I called my client, shared my opinion, which essentially agreed with the plaintiff's two security experts, and, as a consequence, was unable to support my client's theory of defense. I withdrew from the assignment.

SENIOR CITIZEN'S CLAIM, LETTER OF DEMAND

The chief counsel of a major grocery store chain phoned one day advising he received a letter from an attorney representing an elderly lady arrested for shoplifting from one of the chain's markets. He said he was aware of my reputation and expertise and was calling to see if I was available and interested in assisting in the defense of the store. This is typically how an expertise witness is approached in a prospective retention.

I asked him what happened in the store to cause the lawyer to write, as such type of letter is typically the prelude to filing a formal complaint.

The counselor asked, based on what he knew at this early stage, if the shoplifter was detained because she had stolen a pack of cigarettes by slipping it down her dress to conceal it in her bosom. She was escorted up the stairs of the store to the manager's office for the purpose of being processed prior to the police being summoned.

The climb up the stairs was rather difficult for the lady because of her age as well as her asthma, and they had to stop a couple times for her to get her breath and use her inhaler. In the office the proper paperwork was completed and the police were called. They arrived and issued the customer a citation to appear in court.

"How old is the lady?" I asked.

"The attorney claims she's 87 years old," he replied.

"That's pretty old for shoplifting, but it happens, obviously. I'm even surprised the police cited her. What's the issue here?" I asked.

The counselor replied, "The attorney said his client is claiming excessive use of force?"

"What kind of force?" I asked.

"He claims the application of handcuffs was the excessive use of force."

"Handcuffed!? Why in the world was she handcuffed?"

"Well, it's corporate policy. All detainees are handcuffed for the protection of the loss prevention personnel and to deter escape. To avoid claims of discrimination we handcuff everybody—black, white, male, female, young, or old—we handcuff every person in our custody. Standard procedure."

"How much is the attorney demanding?" I asked.

"Nineteen thousand dollars," he replied.

"Pay it," I said, "and the store is getting off easy. A jury would be incensed to see an 87-year-old woman in iron handcuffs. Who would she hurt? How could she possibly run away and escape? In my view, good common sense wasn't used, despite the policy. I wouldn't help defend this matter for twice my fees. Your people are off base and you should see to it the policy is changed to be a little more flexible. That's my opinion and it's free."

"Thank you sir," he replied. "And you're welcome to bill us for your advice."

"No need. Thanks for your interest in my service and the call."

It's been said that civil litigation is simply another strategy for the redistribution of wealth. In some measure, that's true, and regrettably suing often evokes a rather negative reaction. Actually the process, assuming the cause of action (i.e., the reason for the lawsuit) is genuinely justified, and the decision maker (judge or jury) objectively weighs the evidence, provides an essential corrective mechanism necessary in the course of human affairs. The same is true with criminal litigation and the ultimate decision to incarcerate a rapist, for example, in prison. So litigation provides a correction to a condition that can and does bring harm and punishes those responsible for the condition.

Here's an example: A woman is accosted in a dark parking lot. One significant contributing factor to this crime is poor illumination allowing the assailant to hide in the darkness and wait for a victim. The lawsuit stimulates the owner or property manager of the lot to increase and enhance the lighting, according to published recommended lighting engineer's standards, and future attacks are diminished. So now the dangerous condition is somewhat corrected and it's a safer environment for others. That same lawsuit awards some monetary compensation to the victim for her medical expenses, loss of work, and pain and suffering. That monetary award will never erase the memory of the event or future nightmares, but it does ease the pain a bit.

Consider the retailer who doesn't want to incur the costs of training new store detectives. They bypass this necessary requirement and substitute structured and classroom instructions on such topics as the proper use of force, the laws of arrest, etc. with assigning the novice to work alongside an "experienced" detective and call it on-the-job training. Everything the more experienced detective does wrong, or the shortcuts that he or she takes that bypass the rules, are passed on to the newcomer. Later, an innocent person is arrested and jailed, or is injured while being arrested, or worst yet, is killed, albeit accidentally in an arrest or attempted arrest. Some stores have paid dearly for that poorly advised strategy, but only because of civil lawsuits, not because of conscience.

In the Introduction readers learned expert witnesses enjoy a special privilege to offer opinions to the court and jury. That privilege is based on one's credentials in terms of education and experience. Regrettably, there those who hold themselves out as experts, but they're not. Honorable attorneys have a special duty to ensure the expert is honest and credible, but not all attorneys are honorable.

One must wonder, how does the expert arrive at his or her opinion? The answer is by analysis of all available material relevant to the incident that drives a lawsuit. Take, for example, the Elanta Department Store rape case as reflected in Chapter 11. I was obliged to read the following reports and documents, which required days of work:

1. Plaintiff's first amended complaint
2. Newspaper clippings
3. Depositions of Fred Makin, vols. 1 and 2
4. Letter from Attorney Boman
5. Deposition of Clint Roemheld
6. Statement under oath of Thomas Last
7. Plaintiff's second amended complain
8. Copies of colored photographs
9. Items from the prosecutor's file
10. Public record documents from the city
11. Jason Peters personnel file from Sears
12. Jason Peters criminal transcript
13. Elanta's video monitoring procedures
14. Elanta's rules and procedures for security personnel
15. Elanta's management apprehension guide
16. Confirmation that no job description exists
17. Silver's emails regarding camera operations
18. Incident reports involving camera operators
19. Elanta's insurance and safety manual
20. Elanta's file on Jason Peters
21. Hours for security and camera operators
22. Two videotapes (one for training and one of the incident)
23. Oregon's revised codes
24. Deposition of Catherine Stoops
25. Pages of Fred Makin's reviews
26. Pages of Fred Makin's appraisals
27. Oregon's criminal code
28. Defendant's motion for summary judgment
29. Affidavit of Steve McCune
30. Affidavit of Joseph McDonald
31. Affidavit of Buster Kelley

32. Affidavit of Charles Wong
33. Daniel's letter of resignation
34. Chapter 309, Oregon Jury Instructions
35. Chapter 2935
36. Numerous personal statement reports
37. Deposition of Pam Zimmerman
38. Deposition of Sidney Dent
39. Store operations quick reference guide
40. Memo written by Robert's regarding badges
41. Clinton's memo to store managers dated 5/1/2000

At some point the expert forms and offers an opinion. Some opinions are made known in the deposition testimony. Many states require the expert to express his or her opinions in writing, as evidenced as follows in one of six opinions I made about the Elanta case:

As a consequence of my review of all the aforesaid materials and my knowledge and understanding of the industry's standard of care and widely accepted custom and practice, I have arrived at the following opinions:

Opinion #1: Elanta's senior management's failure to appoint and maintain at the senior level a loss prevention executive to develop and administer a professional security/loss prevention program allowed for an unqualified party to develop poorly conceived strategies and policies, which is a reckless disregard for the protection of life and property and falls well below the industry's standard of care.

This expert knows of no other national or even regional retailer who does not have a security executive at the senior or middle management level of the enterprise. Loss prevention is a distinct discipline that plays an integral role in retail operations, comparable to visual presentations, distribution, merchandising, buying, and auditing, each of which brings experience and expertise to their particular phase of the overall function. A company would never put an auditor in charge of visual presentations and displays, nor would a security executive fare well as a buyer of lingerie.

I have worked "both sides of the aisle" in this "litigation explosion" and can fairly take the position that I and a handful of professional colleagues have contributed in some small way to making our communities a safer place to live by bring about improved security.

A Fair Warning: Avoid Victimization

Readers should carry away a fair understanding of how crime impacts our society in general, and, more importantly, its devastating (if not fatal) effect on victims and their loved ones. Let's look at crime this way: there's a lot of it, and every crime has at least one victim.

What does this mean? Table A.1 shows part of the data published by the U.S. Department of Justice every year in a vast annual study titled "Crime in the United States." The data is condensed into what is referred to as the "crime clock."

SUGGESTIONS TO DISCOURAGE, REDUCE, OR PREVENT CRIMES

Murder

In a business environment:

1. Comply with robbers demands for money, don't resist or argue.
2. Report threats of violence in the workforce.
3. Carefully screen who you hire.
4. Provide a well-illuminated place for employees to park.

Table A.1 Data from the "Crime Clock"

Every	Crime
22.2 seconds	One violent crime
30.9 minutes	One murder
5.7 minutes	One forcible rape
1.2 minutes	One robbery
36.6 seconds	One aggravated assault
3.2 seconds	One property crime
14.4 seconds	One burglary
4.8 seconds	One larceny/theft
26.4 seconds	One motor vehicle theft

As an individual:

1. Avoid the lifestyle and people where drugs are involved.
2. Drive your vehicle in a manner not to provoke other motorists.
3. Avoid bars and nightclubs that have a reputation for violence.
4. Comply with an individual with a gun who confronts you and demands your money and valuables.

Rape

In a business environment:

1. A female shouldn't close the business alone at night.
2. A female shouldn't open a business early in the morning when it's still dark outside.
3. A female employee shouldn't leave the business and walk to her car alone after dark; walk in pairs or in a group.
4. If one female must work alone at night, there should be an obvious security presence in the form of CCTV cameras, alarms, and appropriate signage indicating security measures are in place.

As an individual:

1. Avoid walking alone in dark parking areas.
2. Park in busy, heavily trafficked, well-illuminated areas, preferably under light stanchions.
3. Always lock your car.
4. Carry car keys in your hand for prompt entry.
5. If you feel threatened while in a parking area, active your auto alarm with your remote.
6. Lock the doors once inside the car.
7. If being persistently followed by another car, drive to a well-illuminated busy business and use your cellphone to call the police. Or drive to a police station.
8. Don't respond to private or personal classified ads by yourself, especially in remote areas.
9. If at home, ensure your exterior doors are locked, preferably with a deadbolt.
10. If at home, never leave windows or glass sliders fully open at night for ventilation. Locking devises are available to allow partial opening only that are not wide enough for entry by a person. If no lock is available, use a stick or shortened broom handle in the sliding track.
11. If at home, don't open the door without knowing who is ringing or knocking.

12. Don't accept single dates with strangers or men you don't know well, irrespective of how nice or well-groomed he may appear.

13. Be moderate in your alcohol intake while at private parties or clubs.

14. In a hotel, do not open or insert the card key (or any key) to open your door if anyone is walking in the hall close to you. A common crime practice is for a perpetrator to push the guest into her room and then have the privacy to do as he pleases.

15. Do not throw the bolt or swing the privacy latch to prevent the hotel door from fully closing as you go for ice or to visit another room.

Robbery

In a business environment:

1. In a cash business, do not allow the register or terminal to exceed a predetermined amount. Pull out the excess cash and deposit it in drop-safe or other repository designed for that purpose.

2. In the event of a robbery, train employees to promptly comply with the demands.

3. The company safe should be locked at all times.

4. If possible, large sums of money shouldn't be kept at the business but rather should be deposited at the bank.

5. Armored car service is best for transporting cash to the bank.

6. If daily receipts are hand-carried to the bank, the employee should not follow a scheduled time, or routinely follow the same route.

7. Avoid openly carrying bank or deposit bags. Disguise the container so your intention is not conspicuous (e.g., I once carried $1,000,000 in cash and checks to a bank in a sanitary napkin carton).

As an individual:

1. Do not carry large sums of money as a general rule.

2. Do not "flash" or count money when you leave the bank.

3. Don't "flash" or count money openly at an amusement park, race track, or in a casino.

4. At night, avoid parking in poorly illuminated areas.

5. As you drive, keep your car's doors locked.

6. If you have an automatic garage door opener, when you drive into your garage at night, close the garage door before you get out of your car.

7. If approached by a robber, surrender quickly anything he or she demands.

8. As stated before, when staying in a hotel, do not open or insert the card key (or any key) to open your door if anyone is walking in the hall close to you. A common crime practice is for perpetrators to push guests into their rooms and then have the privacy therein to do as they please.

9. In a hotel room, if you receive a call an employee is on their way to deliver something, confirm that call by calling the front desk.

10. Do not throw the bolt or swing the privacy latch to prevent the hotel door from fully closing as you go for ice or to visit another room.

Important tools or weapons of self-defense are the awareness of the potential for crime and the skill of reading body language. *Repeat: awareness and reading body language.*

Here's a practical example of reading body language: A person who is considering doing something bad tends to concentrate on the object of his attack—that is, the victim, if the intention is to harm a person, or an object, if the intention is to steal property. In addition to focusing his or her attention, the individual tends to exhibit some nervousness and project what I have identified as an "aura of guilt" before, during, and subsequent to the crime. Have you ever seen a person "look" guilty when questioned about something he or she shouldn't have done? Have you ever seen a person jump or jerk when you come upon him or her and he or she appears nervous or sheepish and you wondered why? Have you ever seen a person stutter or stammer when not telling the truth? Those are physical manifestations of the sense of guilt—the aura of guilt. A seasoned store detective can tell you his or her experience when he or she has come around a corner and are unexpectedly face to face with a person who has just stolen an item; that eye-to-eye contact with the guilty party evokes an almost visible admission of guilt.

A quick glance at people around you typically reveals everyone is focused on any number of other things, not you. Put another way: look for people looking at you. Practice looking for this and adopt this as your own safety routine. If you feel the slightest bit uneasy because of anyone's presence, break the momentum of the event by reversing your direction or walk toward and close to anyone else in the area until your sense of concern has passed or the person you were wary of is gone. Don't end up a victim. Don't end up in court. Better safe than sorry.

Good luck. Be alert. Be wary. Be safe. Stay safe.

INDEX

Printed and bound by CPI Group (UK) Ltd, Croydon, CR0 4YY

08/06/2025

01896868-0006